ORWELL'S FADED LION

The Moral Atmosphere of Britain
1945–2015

ANTHONY JAMES

ia

imprint-academic.com

Copyright © Anthony James, 2015

The moral rights of the author have been asserted.
No part of this publication may be reproduced in any form
without permission, except for the quotation of brief passages
in criticism and discussion.

Published in the UK by
Imprint Academic, PO Box 200, Exeter EX5 5YX, UK

Distributed in the USA by
Ingram Book Company,
One Ingram Blvd., La Vergne, TN 37086, USA

ISBN 9781845407582

A CIP catalogue record for this book is available from the
British Library and US Library of Congress

**To Emma Anne and the future
and
to the memory of Pamela, 1944–2014**

'The yes-man is your enemy, but your friend will argue with you.'
— Russian Proverb

'Certainly then that people must needs be mad or strangely infatuated, that build the chief hope of their common happiness or safety on a single person; who, if he happen to be good, can do no more than another man; if to be bad, hath in his hands to do more evil without check, than millions of other men. The happiness of a nation must needs be firmest and certainest in full and free council of their own electing, where no single person, but reason only, sways.'
— John Milton

Contents

Chapter One: 'Who Controls the Past Controls the Future' 1

Chapter Two: The Dragon in the Garage 64

Chapter Three: The Monarchy, 'Stick with Nurse...' 78

Chapter Four: The Vacancy is Filled 94

Chapter Five: The Spaniard, the Brazilian, the Russian and the German 127

Afterword: Liver Disease and Sociology 137

Index 149

Chapter One

'Who Controls the Past Controls the Future'

Tolstoy began his novel *Anna Karenina* with the famous line: 'All happy families resemble one another, but each unhappy family is unhappy in its own way.' Perhaps we can usefully paraphrase Tolstoy's statement: all humane societies resemble one another, but each inhumane and unjust society is inhumane and unjust in its own way.

When the *Daily Mail* attacked the father of the leader of the Labour Party in autumn 2013, the paper also had something to say about the historian Eric Hobsbawm. The father of the Labour leader had been called 'the man who hated Britain' by the *Daily Mail*, which then added a 'postscript' on Hobsbawm's 'refusal to condemn Stalinism's 30 million dead or the brutal Soviet invasion of Hungary in 1956'. These statements about Hobsbawm are lies. Hobsbawm calls the millions of deaths under Stalin 'shameful and beyond palliation, let alone justification', as well as reprinting a collective letter of protest against the Soviet invasion, co-signed by himself, in his autobiography.[1]

Not surprisingly, the Labour leader dismissed the accusation made against his father as false, and yet hatred is difficult to prove or measure, whereas anyone can open Hobsbawm's enduringly popular books and see the proof of this newspaper's dishonesty in black and white. Sadly, it is safe to assume that very, very few of the *Daily Mail's* readers ever did so. The paper also told its readers that Marxism supplied the 'philosophical underpinning' of Stalinism (presumably just as the teachings of Jesus supplied the philosophical underpinning for the burning of heretics and 'witches' by the Christian Church), although those who wrote this did not show the least sign that they had even a faint understanding of either Marxism or Stalinism.

Perhaps we could also consider the following before we move on. There are two photographs (Agence France Presse) of Saddam Hussein, then friend and ally of the West, visiting southern France in September 1975 in order to buy weapons. There is another photograph (Getty Images) of his body, just after he was hastily judicially murdered, published on 31 December 2006. It is difficult not to think of one of the most celebrated passages from Orwell's *Nineteen Eighty-Four* in connection with these photographs: '…at just this moment it had been announced that Oceania was not after all at war with Eurasia. Oceania was at war with Eastasia. Eurasia was an ally.' Of course, we do not yet live in a world governed by a ruling elite motivated by the lust for pure power, such as the one in Orwell's novel. America and Britain supplied Saddam with the chemical weapons and intelligence used to carry out some of his worst war crimes and atrocities. This was done out of a monumental greed for profit; and any lie—however cynical or fantastic—can and will be used to conceal that motivation.

British and Western governments rarely ban books or simply destroy information and then go forward with the conviction that such information has never existed (which was the method of the Party in Orwell's novel). And yet these governments understand very well the Party's slogan in *Nineteen Eighty-Four*: 'Who controls the past controls the future: who controls the present controls the past.' The dishonest speeches of politicians seem to be greeted increasingly with healthy scepticism and cynicism by ordinary people. However, alongside such utterances there is the much more potent and seductive stream of superficiality and bigotry served up by the popular press. The abundance of information available today has to some extent made all of us indifferent and numb. There is something unreal about *'Lasers in the jungle somewhere / Staccato signals of constant information / A loose affiliation of millionaires and billionaires'* as Paul Simon called them in his 1986 song *The Boy in the Bubble*. The popular press prods very effectively on the nerves of fear and resentment in communities saturated with information and weary of facts and more facts. We shall return to the activities of the tabloid press and to war in the Middle East further on. However, we need to contemplate the road Britain has travelled since Orwell wrote so perceptively about this country, spelling out his hopes for change in *The Lion and the Unicorn* as the Nazi bombs fell. The examples of 'news' and 'information' given above are sadly relevant to the history of the last seventy years.

A Labour government was elected with a large majority in July 1945 with Clement Attlee as Prime Minister, proceeding to create the National Health Service and nationalize the coal, electricity, gas and steel industries as well as transport; this was rather far from the left-wing, non-communist revolution that Orwell had in mind. Nationalization in itself was not enough, indeed meant very little, without a change in culture, as Orwell knew only too well. The culture of equality and the culture of democracy need to be developed in a revolution that is a process and not a single event — something that was impossible to create in besieged, starving, backward Soviet Russia after 1917 and something not really attempted in Britain after 1945.

The British class system and social structure were left largely untouched after the war, and elements of them remain surprisingly resilient and tenacious today. Nevertheless, as the television journalist and 1960s icon Joan Bakewell described in her autobiography *The Centre of the Bed* (2003), the early years of the new Labour government were generally a time of optimism and idealism. It was not to last. The general election of May 1950 cut the large Labour majority to five. The war had created the momentum for the electoral landslide of 1945, but its aftermath spread disillusionment with Labour as people reacted against continuing austerity. The Conservatives led by Churchill returned to office, the Labour Party being subsequently defeated in the general elections of 1951, 1955 and 1959. The Cold War began in 1947, although this was to a large extent a corner into which Truman (and, to a lesser extent, Churchill in his 1946 'Iron Curtain' speech) had backed Stalin, as a realistic consideration of events reveals.

The reappraisal of Stalin as a leader by the widely respected historian Geoffrey Roberts is more generous to the Soviet dictator than the account by Hobsbawm, a member of the Communist Party for fifty years.[2] In any case, the Cold War could only make people more conservative and defensive and make the Conservatives more popular, as—in part at least—it was designed to do. The crisis over the Falkland Islands in 1982 and the war against a distant and much weaker enemy had something of the same effect thirty-five years later. Still, the acceptance of the need for full employment and a welfare state by all the major political parties *did* endure until the mid-1970s when the post-war consensus was torn up by Margaret Thatcher and the alliance of social and political forces that she represented. The consensus was helped by the period of prosperity that was already underway when Anthony Eden became Prime Minister in 1955.

It was Eden who led Britain to the next decisive break with the optimism of 1945, a watershed in the mental and social atmosphere of British society. (I was born in 1956 at the beginning of the Suez Crisis and during the Hungarian National Rising, and it has always amused me that I was named after Anthony Eden by my—at that time—right-wing parents, no doubt as a defensive reflex in denial of Eden's disastrous leadership, rather as the central character of Orwell's *Nineteen Eighty-Four*, who was a very young child in 1945, was named Winston Smith.)

Just over a quarter of a century after Suez and Hungary, on 16 June 1982, the *Guardian* declared that historians must judge how the war in the Falklands must be seen in 'the annals of Britain's post-1945 adjustment to her reduced circumstances as a declining power'. The answer may be that the British have never really made this adjustment and have failed to do so in surprising ways. The British ruling class had certainly made no such accommodation with reality by 1956 when President Nasser of Egypt nationalized the Suez Canal Company. Eden, the once cool and self-assured Foreign Secretary, widely admired for these qualities, crazily perceived Nasser as a leader in the Hitler mould (it is hardly stretching a point to recall that journalists have sometimes ignorantly stated that Saddam Hussein was similar to Stalin). Britain and France colluded with an Israeli attack on Egypt beginning on 29 October, of which they had secret knowledge, attacked the Egyptians from the air on 31 October and landed troops near Port Said on 5 November 1956.

A great deal of anger and disgust was aroused among the British public at home by the invasion, which also provoked the resolute and outspoken hostility of the UN, America, Canada and several Commonwealth countries. The Soviet Union supported Egypt and threatened Britain and France with nuclear war (although the Russians almost certainly did not seriously contemplate it).[3] The hard lesson was driven home: Britain and France were no longer strong enough to defy the Americans actively or defy the Soviets and the UN without American support. Of course, *with* American encouragement British Prime Ministers could later act out Britain-as-Great-Power fantasies in order to sway public opinion and—presumably—satisfy their own quirks and prejudices. In 1956, however, the sorry Anglo-French military fiasco was effectively ended on 7 November, and Eden's reputation was destroyed, leading to his resignation in January 1957, as despised as a Prime Minister after twenty-one months in office as he had once been admired as a Foreign Secretary.

The Suez Crisis unfolded at exactly the same time as the Soviet invasion of Hungary and the suppression of the Hungarian National Rising, an event that has passed into right-wing legend in Britain and still provides the popular press with useful propaganda material today. As usual with events of such importance, what happened in Hungary is not well understood; to point this out is not to deny the sufferings of the Hungarians or to pretend that the Soviets acted with any shred of morality. The Russians based their actions on strategic expediency — nothing more and nothing less. The Soviet interest in Eastern Europe generally was always strategic, and this was originally accepted with some sympathy by both Churchill and Roosevelt. Stalin was at first content with multi-party systems in Eastern European countries as long as these led to broadly left leaning governments that were friendly to the Soviet Union; his tactics and strategy changed to the imposition of monolithic 'people's democracies' in the states bordering the Soviet Union only after Truman initiated the Cold War in his speech to Congress on 12 March 1947. If Stalin was paranoid, President Truman's foreign policy and the vast loss of life and devastation caused by Hitler's war on Russia convinced him that he had a great deal to be paranoid about. Even then, the actual developments in countries on the Soviet Union's western borders were very different from the Cold War legends accepted in Britain.

The Czechoslovak Communist Party still had the support of forty per cent of the electorate when it took power in February 1948, although the public mood in Czechoslovakia had been hardening against the communists for some months; there were no Soviet troops in the country at that time and the Party took power by its own efforts. Czechs and Slovaks generally felt a great deal of friendly loyalty towards Russia, which had been prepared to go to war to defend Czechoslovakia against Hitler in 1938 and 1939, whereas Britain and France sold them to the Nazis. Stalin's demand that Finland sign a mutual assistance treaty with the Soviet Union made at the same time as the communist takeover in Prague was seen as part of the same inexorable advance of the evil Soviet empire. The fact that the Finns stubbornly refused to sign anything beyond a limited defensive treaty concerned with an attack by a resurgent Germany — as well as retaining a Western democratic system and pursuing a neutral foreign policy — was conveniently brushed aside.[4]

When the Hungarians rose against the hated communist leadership and secret police in their country, their discontent intensified by a bad harvest and fuel shortages, Soviet troops began to withdraw from Hungary in deference to the mass demonstrations on 23 October. The new Hungarian government allowed the old political parties to be re-formed and included their representatives in the administration of the country. The Russians seemed likely to accept these arrangements, if only reluctantly. The breaking point came when the Hungarian leaders announced that Hungary would withdraw from the Warsaw Pact and become a neutral nation like Switzerland and Austria. The Soviet tanks returned to Hungary and began the brutal suppression of the rising on 4 November, the day before the British and French invaded Egypt, and four days *after* planes from Britain and France attacked the Egyptians.

It is possible that international protest and pressure could have compelled the Russians to retreat or make concessions, but the British and French action served both to legitimize the use of force by the Soviets and distract attention from Hungary. Eden's ill-advised and unrealistic war-making sealed the fate of Hungary just as Chamberlain's appeasement of Hitler had sealed the fate of Czechoslovakia and Truman's naïve and inexperienced bellicosity had established the Cold War. It is not surprising that right-wing politicians and newspapers from Margaret Thatcher to the *Daily Mail* astutely ignored—and continue to avoid mentioning—the intimate connection between Suez and Hungary, concentrating instead on their belief that 'Marxism supplied the philosophical underpinning to a monstrously evil regime', as the *Mail* put it on 1 October 2013, echoing President Reagan and others.

'A man may take to drink because he feels himself to be a failure, and then fail all the more completely because he drinks.' Orwell remarked in *Politics and the English Language* (1946), '...the English language becomes ugly and inaccurate because our thoughts are foolish, but the slovenliness of our language makes it easier for us to have foolish thoughts... if thought corrupts language, language can also corrupt thought'. Of course, as Orwell would have agreed, what else is there to be done in a world that produces Egyptian Hitlers except make war on Egyptian Hitlers, ignoring the fact that you are helping a monstrously evil empire? One of your successors then takes care of the home front by suppressing members of the 'Fascist Left', such as coalminers, and their ungovernable activities until the evil empire is good and dead. It then remains for *her* successors to wage a War on Terror against an Iraqi Stalin, whose weapons of mass destruction (comfortingly labelled WMD) inconveniently cannot be found, which is all the more frustrating as she was ready enough to sell the things to him in the first place—even to the point of refusing to dissuade him from hanging a Western journalist in case that interfered with the deal.

Although Suez destroyed Eden politically, he was far from solely responsible for the debacle, and the role played by other members of his cabinet showed a political nastiness that has become so familiar these days that we hardly notice it. David Runciman has written a full length study of Blair's policy and motivations, but he also provides a fascinating analysis of Suez and the similarities and differences between that crisis and the invasion of Iraq.

> It was Macmillan who did most to persuade Eden that an Anglo-French invasion of Egypt... was a gamble worth taking ... Yet it was also Macmillan who pulled the plug on the invasion after less than a week, when he told the cabinet that he could not stem a run on the pound... Macmillan revealed himself to be a born risk taker... so long as the stakes were not his own... Macmillan was as responsible as anyone for the disaster of Suez.[5]

It was Macmillan, of course, who replaced Eden after his resignation in January 1957. Blair did not resign when no weapons of mass destruction were uncovered in Iraq and it became even more glaringly obvious than before that the war was simply about President Bush's appetite for a change of regime in that country: the days of resignation over a point of honour and an acceptance of responsibility were by then long gone in Britain. Still, we can only wonder which of Blair's nimble but pro-war colleagues might have taken his job if he had resigned.

Suez did not create the sense of disillusionment and discontent among young people in Britain in the mid-1950s, but it certainly accelerated and crystallized it. A generation with only childhood or adolescent memories of the Second World War, having taken no direct part in that war, had grown up.

A revolution in the British theatre occurred on 8 May 1956, a few months before Suez and Hungary, when *Look Back in Anger* by John Osborne was first performed at the Royal Court Theatre in London; the play was a signal of what was in the air — a function that literature so often fulfils. The 1958 film version with Richard Burton — at his miraculous best — as Jimmy Porter, the central character of the play, probably best conveys the excitement and vitality of the original work, although it sometimes strays from the dramatic text. 'There aren't any good, brave causes left', says Jimmy Porter, 'If the big bang does come, and we all get killed off, it won't be in aid of the old-fashioned, grand design. It'll just be for the Brave New-nothing-very-much-thank-you. About as pointless and inglorious as stepping in front of a bus.' We are too far removed in time from the 'good, brave causes' for any writer of today to express Jimmy Porter's (and Osborne's) outrage; today that kind of outrage would sound merely quaint. One outstanding piece of British literature published in 2012 expresses anger of a rather different kind. A later chapter of this book will focus on the way in which our post-1945 history has been reflected in literature.

Britain in the 1950s was involved in conflict in Kenya as well as in Egypt, once again exercising its power — or fulfilling its responsibilities as some would say — on the continent of Africa. It should be said that the Mau Mau secret society in Kenya killed a great many Africans, although it was dedicated to driving out White colonialists. Nevertheless, the scale of the internment of members of the Kikuyu tribe as a result of British policy has emerged only in recent years. The conditions at the Hola prison camp in which eleven Mau Mau prisoners died in March 1959 was condemned in Parliament by Enoch Powell in a speech on 27 July 1959, a fact that may surprise those familiar only with his later statements on racial issues. Powell declared:

> [I]t is a fearful doctrine, which must recoil upon the heads of those who pronounce it... We cannot say, 'We will have African standards in Africa, Asian standards in Asia and perhaps British standards here at home.'... We must be consistent with ourselves everywhere. All Government, all influence of man upon man, rests upon opinion... depends upon the opinion which is entertained of the way in which this country acts and the way in which Englishmen act.

And what about British standards 'here at home' in recent times?

There were several arrests in London and Leicester in December 2001 and January 2002, and although the people arrested were not charged they were imprisoned in Belmarsh, the high security prison in London. They were kept in their cells for twenty-two hours a day without seeing daylight, having no contact with their families or with lawyers and without prayer facilities — except for fifteen minutes a week without an imam present. Gareth Peirce, a solicitor who represented some of the prisoners, has been quoted as saying: 'these men have been buried alive in concrete coffins and have been told the legislation provides for their detention for life without trial.' These details come from an essay by Philip A. Thomas, Professor of Law, Cardiff Law School, Cardiff University, and Editor of *Journal of Law and Society*.[6] Enoch Powell's later warnings and prophecies have been justifiably dismissed with derision — riots and 'rivers of blood' have too often been outbursts from people of different racial backgrounds acting together. Yet how clearly his warning from 1959 echoes down the decades to the present day!

The way in which the Amritsar massacre committed by British troops in India in April 1919 was broadly tolerated by the British public was understandable at that time; sensibilities were less developed and news did not instantly reach all levels of society. Further, as Orwell pointed out in both *The Lion and the Unicorn* and in his essay on Rudyard Kipling, the majority of the British people before the Second World War were anti-militarist but bored by the Empire, while the peculiarities of British politics—as well as any national tendency towards holding a double-faced attitude—made hypocrisy towards Britain's imperial policy all the easier. The situation was vastly different in all these ways by the 1950s. Egypt had long been an independent state when the British and French attacked it and the nations of Africa were moving towards post-colonial political (if not economic) independence. Thus, imperialist actions became increasingly corrupt and corrupting. The involvement of British soldiers in morally equivocal wars that required lies to justify them over the six decades since the 1950s has changed the mental atmosphere of Britain.

The Conservatives led by Harold Macmillan won the election of 1959 on the slogan 'You've never had it so good', an assertion— unusual among party political declarations—that was admittedly true. The upheaval of Suez was receding into the past and the forces of the establishment looked more firmly established than ever, helped by the economic boom and stable prices in the first years after the election.

Jimmy Porter's tirades crashed out from British stages in Osborne's perennially popular play: there was much about which to rant with indignation, but very little seemed to change. Of course, the prosperity was not confined to Britain, because this was the Golden Age of capitalism, as historians and economists would later call it.[7] 'Mass unemployment? Where was it to be found in the developed world in the 1960s…?', Eric Hobsbawm asks in *Age of Extremes*:

> Poverty? Of course, most of humanity remained poor, but… what meaning could the *Internationale's* 'Arise, ye starvelings from your slumbers' have for workers who now expected to have their car and spend their annual paid vacation on the beaches of Spain? And, if they fell upon hard times, would not… the Welfare State provide them with protection…?

Unemployment *did* rise in Britain as the years passed under Macmillan's government, and British governments of the 1960s and 1970s were plagued and obsessed by uncertainty over the balance of payments: the economic problems seemed serious enough at the time. And yet — as ever in history — we can see the real nature of the Golden Age in retrospect, looking back from the era of crisis that has followed the end of that Age in about 1973. Yet there were telltale signs of a change in the cultural and political air in Britain even while Macmillan was Prime Minister, and two of them were oddly connected with sex — a subject that bothers the British, or at least the British establishment, to this day.

In 1960, a judgement in a court of law found that D.H. Lawrence's novel *Lady Chatterley's Lover* was not obscene, despite the fact that it had been banned for nearly thirty years. Clearly, this turning point affected the content of much of literature and the cultural atmosphere generally. (British society has always been at its most depressingly immature in its inquisitorial outbursts over the sexual or alleged anti-religious nature of serious books, films, or even light entertainment. But it is rather sad that *Lady Chatterley's Lover* is not a better novel; it is clear that it is a manifesto-tract from the first page. The sex scenes in the book may describe sex as a 'holy communion', as one witness said in court in its defence, but the descriptions are sometimes rather unconvincing.)

It was not sex between characters on the pages of a novel but rather sex between real people that accelerated dislike of the Macmillan government in the spring of 1963. A cabinet minister named John Profumo was having a relationship with a woman called Christine Keeler, who was said to be intimate with a Soviet naval attaché. Profumo felt it was necessary to lie to the House of Commons about this relationship, admitting that he had lied just over two months later and resigning from the cabinet and from Parliament. As an official inquiry later found that Profumo's sex life had not caused a breach of national security, we can imagine that a government minister in some countries would have insisted on this as the only relevant fact and otherwise told the truth, but in Britain the establishment's preoccupation with sex swiftly rebounded on one of its members. Predictably, the newspapers feasted on the scandal, while Macmillan seemed to be taken unawares by the matter, or (which would be more to his credit) was too urbane to take any great interest in it.

Macmillan had problems of his own, and his bad health led him to resign in October 1963. The largely unknown Alec Douglas-Home became Prime Minister for a year (when he was recommended to Churchill for the post of Minister for Scotland in 1951, Churchill is said to have growled, 'Never heard of him'). Harold Wilson led the Labour Party to a narrow victory in the 1964 election—a parliamentary majority of only five—although he acted with considerable political nerve, governing as if he had a large majority and refusing to make concessions over policy or any coalition-minded advances towards the Liberals.

Wilson seemed to stand for a new, modern politics, projecting something of the 'Camelot' quality (civilized, liberal, optimistic leadership and renewal) that the media had attached to President Kennedy's White House. Wilson had also astutely posed for a photograph as he chatted to The Beatles at a Show Business Awards ceremony in London on 19 March 1964. Fortunately for Labour, the honeymoon lasted for the next seventeen months until Wilson chose to call a general election for the end of March 1966, increasing his majority to ninety-nine seats.

The sociologist Krishan Kumar suggests a lengthy list of cultural figures and features that forms a mosaic of sixties Britain, all marked with 'some aspect of the mood of irreverence, ridicule, rebellion, novelty and of the general effort to throw off all "artificial" and antiquated constraints, and to "do your own thing"'. The list includes the pop music of The Beatles, The Rolling Stones and The Who; the fashion designs of Mary Quant; the models, actresses and actors Jean Shrimpton, Twiggy, Julie Christie, Albert Finney, Michael Caine, Terence Stamp; satirical comedy such as *Beyond the Fringe*; the magazine *Private Eye*; the new television full-time professional personalities, created by TV (I add this distinction, although Kumar does not) such as David Frost; the spy novels of John Le Carre (enlarging upon Kumar's list, I would point out the high literary quality of Le Carre's books in comparison to the even more famous books—and their cinematic spin-offs—about the fantasy spy James Bond); films, television plays and documentaries such as *Alfie, Darling, Cathy Come Home, Up the Junction*; television drama series such as *Z Cars* and *The Avengers*; 'permissiveness' in sexual attitudes and 'progressiveness' in education.[8]

All in all, for those too young to remember the sixties—and even for some of those who do remember those years—the decade sometimes seems more remote than the Victorian England of Dickens and George Eliot. Yet despite the new culture and the judgement in the *Lady Chatterley* trial in 1960, and no doubt also because of them, a schoolteacher named Mary Whitehouse began her campaign against the explicit and the obscene on television and radio in 1964, and 'expressed the fears of middle England [without] convoluted intellectual dilemmas... she protested from the centre of her own life and attitudes, thousands identified with her', as Joan Bakewell recalls in her autobiography *The Centre of the Bed*. The attitudes of Mrs Whitehouse were stunningly simple-minded, censorious and vindictive, and she predictably did a fair amount of actual harm. We might expect such a person to wield considerable influence in some parts of America, but her influence in Britain in the 1960s and the 1970s is a dreadful comment on the society that was able to take her seriously. Those who express 'the fears of middle England' have demonstrated that they are still very much alive and hissing even today.

A great many of the changes brought about by Wilson's Labour government of 1964–70 were, nevertheless, liberalizing and liberating. The Murder (Abolition of the Death Penalty) Act, 1965, was perpetuated by a free vote in both Houses of Parliament in December 1969. The Family Law Reform Act, 1969, was based on the same recommendations as the Representation of the People Act, 1969, in the matter of voting age, reducing it from twenty-one to eighteen years of age. And previously, in

1967, homosexuality and abortion were made legal within defined limits. (However, capital punishment remained the penalty for treason, technically at least. Or was it entirely a technicality? On 22 October 1975, when Gerry Conlon and the other innocent members of the 'Guildford Four' were convicted of murder and bombing, the judge, Mr Justice (later Lord) Donaldson wondered why they hadn't been charged with treason so that they could be sentenced to death. Harold Wilson was once again Prime Minister at the time of that trial.)[9] It would, of course, be wonderful to remember the 1960s and the Wilson years in Britain as wholly a time of regard for human rights and the defence of freedom, but sadly they were not.

The Wilson government and Wilson personally certainly committed a crime against human rights and international law in its treatment of the people of the island of Diego Garcia in the Chagos archipelago in the Indian Ocean. These people had lived on the islands for several generations, their origins there going back to the eighteenth century. A British Indian Ocean Territory was created on 8 November 1965 by an order of the Privy Council, made up of present and former cabinet ministers and presided over by the Queen. The decision was thus kept secret and not approved by Parliament. Robin Cook, who resigned from Blair's government in March 2003 in protest against the invasion of Iraq, stated to the journalist and film-maker John Pilger that MPs 'knew nothing about it; the keeping of that secret was amazing'.

Democracy Wilson-style was no different from British democracy before or after him. The islanders were expelled by means of terror, and on the orders of Sir Bruce Greatbatch, her Majesty's Governor of the Seychelles, their dogs—particularly loved and revered in their society—were poisoned, left to die in agony, gassed by the exhaust fumes of a truck and many of them burnt while still alive. The islanders were given to understand that they would suffer the same fate and were threatened with bombing by American aircraft.

It was to the Americans that their island was sold in order to create a huge military, naval and air base, with two bomber runways, anchorage for a fleet of ships and luxurious facilities for American personnel. The Chagossians were deported to Mauritius where they lived in terrible poverty and disease well into the twenty-first century, continuing to struggle for the right to go home to Diego Garcia, where they had enjoyed an unusually prosperous, orderly and beautiful—if simple—life.

The British government sold Diego Garcia (and sold the 2,000 inhabitants, who were British citizens, into exile, poverty and death from malnutrition and disease) for the price of a $14 million discount from the cost of a Polaris nuclear submarine. The original contract was signed by Lord Chalfont of the British Foreign Office and the Pentagon in December 1966, the Americans demanding the expulsion of the entire population of the island. Further, the scale of this crime was kept secret by successive British governments—Labour and Conservative—until the 1990s; the criminal nature of the conspiracy is in no doubt, Article 7 of the Statute of the International Criminal Court defines forcible deportation or transfer of a population as a crime against humanity. Article 73 of the UN Charter also calls upon colonial powers (such as Britain) to protect the human rights of dependent peoples.

Presidents Johnson and Nixon also kept the crime a secret from Congress. Also, there is for the British the painful difference between the treatment of the Chagossians and the treatment of the Falkland islanders. The British army and navy went eight thousand miles to defend the 'paramount' wishes of the Falkland islanders at a cost of £2 billion. The Falkland islanders are white, of course, but the Chagossians are black. And yet the consciousness of the British public has barely been touched—if it has been touched at all—by the crime committed by the British establishment in the Chagos archipelago.

This terrible episode has been brought to light by the historical writings of Mark Curtis and the detailed account by John Pilger; the long chapter on the selling of Diego Garcia in a recent book by Pilger has seventy-nine notes upon and references to sources, many of them official. Even in the 1960s, one brave man called George Champion, a schoolteacher from Kent, campaigned single-handedly for the Diego Garcians, even changing his name to 'Chagos'. Pilger likens this campaign to that of Brian Haw who camped in Parliament Square for years in protest against the invasion of Iraq.[10, 11]

There were two secret minutes written by Anthony Greenwood, the Colonial Secretary, to Prime Minister Harold Wilson on 5 and 8 November 1965, urging the Privy Council to order the creation of the British Indian Ocean Territory, separating the Chagos archipelago from the British colony of Mauritius and providing the smokescreen for the ethnic cleansing that followed. The British Foreign Secretary, Michael Stewart, wrote to Wilson on 25 July 1968 suggesting that the government should spread the lie that there was no indigenous population in Diego Garcia. And subsequently, on 26 April 1969, Wilson's private secretary informed Stewart in writing of the Prime Minister's approval; John Pilger provides full references for these communications. Declassified official documents in the National Archives at Kew in south-west London made the scale of the crime in Chagos clear. Despite the complicity of successive British governments in the cover-up, the main responsibility lies with Harold Wilson and his ministers. It was not to be the last time that a Labour Prime Minister and a Labour government would eagerly submit to the worst aspects of American policy. (The forcible uprooting of populations was undeniably a feature of Stalin's regime, which, as the *Daily Mail* reminded us in October 2013, was 'a monstrously evil regime'. The popular tabloid press is rather silent on the subject of Diego Garcia: 'Who controls the past controls the future...')

Through the late sixties and the 1970s the trade unions wielded considerable power and influence in Britain. For the first time 'market forces' and profits were balanced by the needs and demands of ordinary working people. (In case I am suspected of idealizing the trade unions, perhaps I can assure the reader that we will take a look at how their own faults contributed to the eclipse of their influence and to the sharp deterioration in British society after 1979.) The overwhelming majority of trade union members had no wish to bring the capitalist system to an end or take political power themselves, something which all sensible people realized and which some Marxists—sensible or otherwise—could only regret. But as with much else, trade union power excited and inflated 'the fears of middle England'.

The new freedoms of the 1960s and the influence of trade unions either left some sections of society untouched or meant limited advances in comparison to rights that we take for granted today. Women are better off in the early twenty-first century in Britain than they were in the late sixties. To take one example, as recalled by one woman I know very well from her personal experience, getting pregnant at the age of seventeen meant that a young woman had to leave school without even being consulted (in this lady's case she was a flourishing sixth form student taking one of the first courses in computer studies). While in the area of mental health, psychiatric patients —perennially one of society's most oppressed groups—are somewhat better off today. It should be remembered that the psychiatrist William Sargant (1907–1988) carried out experiments on unfortunate patients, such as women suffering from postnatal depression, in London in the 1960s and 1970s, inflicting suffering with an irresponsibility and cruelty as atrocious as that of the Nazi Dr Joseph Mengele at Auschwitz. Sargant's activities in the sixties and seventies were carried out while he was working for the National Health Service, but he began by performing psychological experiments on soldiers evacuated from Dunkirk at a psychiatric unit at Belmont, near Sutton; the politician and former Labour cabinet minister Lord David Owen was Sargant's colleague and still defends him. The full extent of Sargant's assault on the health and liberty of his victims is still being unearthed, thanks to the pioneering efforts of the author, journalist and broadcaster James Maw.[12, 13] And finally, as I well remember, children continued to be subjected to corporal punishment and random acts of violence by teachers, even at grammar schools with a 'good reputation', well into the 1970s.

The sudden upsurge of student radicalism, youth rebellion with a political edge and intellectual ferment in 1968, together with its social reverberations, signalled that the Golden Age of capitalism could not last, although the decisive crash was not to come until 1973-74. There was something in the Golden Age (*not* indignation over crimes like the forcible deportation of the Chagossians or the legalized atrocities of men like William Sargant, which did not come to light until much later) that aroused the hostility of many of the strongest, most intelligent and most sensitive members of society; the way of life of the Golden Age somehow could not satisfy them. The same could be said of capitalism itself: in some way it fails to win over many of its gifted citizens, even—or especially—some privileged members of society who benefit from it greatly. The pattern of outrage in nineteenth-century Russia in men and women like Turgenev, Tolstoy, Vera Zasulich, Alexander Ulyanov (Lenin's elder brother), Nadezhda Krupskaya (Lenin's wife) and then Lenin himself has something like a parallel in America and in Britain in our own day in individuals like Gore Vidal, Noam Chomsky, Jane Fonda, Tony Benn, Germaine Greer and (most recently) J.K. Rowling.

Whether the 'Prague Spring' in Czechoslovakia in 1968 was part of the same wave of radicalism, or a quite separate development within Soviet dominated Eastern Europe that just happened to occur in the same year, is a difficult question to answer. There had been accelerating—and increasingly openly expressed—resentment at the Soviet Union's almost colonial manipulation of the Czechoslovak economy in the two years before the 'Prague Spring', extending to complaints about the absolute power of the Communist Party, the lack of individual freedom and Czech domination of Slovakia. As with Hungary, Czechoslovakia's action programme of reform might in itself have been reluctantly accepted by the Soviets, but once again, as they had in Hungary, the Russians acted brutally upon strategic considerations.

Despite the so-called 'Brezhnev Doctrine' of the Soviet leader at that time, which states that a socialist country has an obligation to intervene in another socialist country if the survival of socialism is threatened, the reality was, as the historian

Alan Palmer so succinctly described it, 'the heirs of Stalin and Khrushchev were no more willing than their predecessors to tolerate a partially open society in a country which formed, geographically, a strategic corridor 370 miles long between American-garrisoned Bavaria and the Ukraine'.[14] The Soviet suppression of reform in Czechoslovakia was not as bitterly harsh as the Soviet invasion of Hungary; there may be something in the argument that it did not need to be as brutal and widespread because the 'Prague Spring' was less of an anti-Soviet national rising and more a movement of intellectuals in the capital city and Slovaks discontented with Czech domination, leaving large sections of the older Czech working class largely loyal to the Soviet Union.

However, like Hungary in 1956, Czechoslovakia in 1968 has passed into British right-wing folklore, which completely ignores the fact that the Czech reform leaders and intellectuals were quite unsympathetic to Western capitalism. Similarly, the Russian dissident writer Solzhenitsyn was the darling of Conservatives and the tabloid press until it became apparent that he held capitalist Britain in as much contempt as he held the Soviet communist leaders. Margaret Thatcher did meet Solzhenitsyn — they had in common a profound hostility to the Soviet leaders, but it is safe to assume that they understood each other very little and thought about each other even less. But in 1968, approval of Solzhenitsyn was common in the British press and also among many left-wing journalists, though for rather different reasons. His courageous opposition to the stagnating Soviet system pleased people of varying political sympathies.

Harold Wilson has sometimes been criticized for failing to foresee the conflict in Northern Ireland, although it seems that— given the nature of the conflict—it was less a failure of foresight and more of an inability to stem the accelerating series of events that had started in the sixties, until those events had reached and passed crisis point. We can now see how vividly the criminal oppression of the Chagossians demonstrates that Wilson was unable or unwilling to rid himself of the fixed concepts, assumptions and prejudices of the British establishment in matters other than domestic reform and domestic policy. Wilson, like the Prime Ministers who succeeded him in the following twenty-five years, lacked the imagination to confront the Northern Ireland situation effectively. A large-scale demonstration by the Civil Rights movement in Derry on 5 October 1968 and the request for British troops made by the Northern Ireland government in Belfast in April 1969 marked points of no return.

A detailed or in-depth account of the civil war that exploded in Northern Ireland is beyond the scope of this book, and yet one point is of urgent concern here. The conflict grew out of conditions of enormous injustice and suffering, and the excesses committed on both sides cannot alter that fact. Ultimately, it is not in itself so very surprising that atrocities took place; war is a brutalizing process for all those involved in it. The lying and distortions of the facts by successive British governments and the press were far more serious and far more corrosive. The conflict was portrayed for years as a religious war, which it was not: it was a civil war driven by social and political issues with a long and bitter history. The Ulster Peace Movement, largely led by women, which was internationally acknowledged by the award of the Nobel Peace Prize to Maire Corrigan and Betty Williams in 1976, readily crossed the Catholic and Protestant divide. Worse still was the demonization of 'the other side' as evil psychopaths who set off bombs and shot innocent people for no reason at all — or perhaps solely to gain power for themselves, excluding everyone else. When peace finally came, members of 'the other side' worked — largely successfully — in coalition with their former enemies.

The dishonest evasion of the fact that the British army was actually fighting people with a point of view, a genuine sense of grievance and outrage and a cause for which they were prepared to die, surely delayed the coming of peace by many years. Instead, the poisonous illusion that the conflict was solely a matter of 'our boys' risking their lives and getting killed to put down demons and degenerates was firmly planted in the minds of ordinary British people over decades. The language of the tabloid press of the *'SAS RUBS OUT IRA RATS'* variety was ugly to the point of being reminiscent of the Nazis. And, as usual in history, the deceivers deceived themselves and became infected by their own deception. This was the mental climate in which the British government used torture in Northern Ireland, and was condemned by Amnesty International for doing so.[15] A fertile mental soil for the post-September 11 2001 world, the 'War on Terror' and 'post-liberal social control' was already being laid down by the Labour and Conservative governments of Harold Wilson and Edward Heath in the 1960s and 1970s.

Surprisingly, the Conservatives won the election in June 1970, although the outlook and way of life of the sixties, which Labour had done a great deal to create, seemed to be still in full swing. Wilson had become increasingly unpopular on a personal level, and his rather unattractive physical appearance, his pipe and his raincoat were easy to ridicule and caricature. Tony Benn and others on the political left have lamented the contemporary obsession with personalities in politics and called it boring—no doubt it is, but it is a very powerful force nonetheless. Part of the success of Margaret Thatcher and Tony Blair lay in the fact that they were physically attractive individuals; Margaret Thatcher's detractors sometimes said that she looked increasingly crazy as the years passed, but looking crazy is not necessarily unattractive.

Wilson was also a victim of his own success. In domestic politics Wilson's premiership *was* a success story, although this was forgotten or denied with extraordinary swiftness after his final departure from office in 1976. The electorate had very little real grievance against Labour in 1970, and Heath and the Conservatives did not offer anything substantially better or indeed very different. But why not, after all? Vote or not vote, and *if* you vote why not try voting *against* Wilson, the man who smoked a pipe, and *for* Heath, the man who sailed a racing yacht? Do your own thing!

The Golden Age was coming to an end by the next general election in 1974, and thereafter governments were once again elected on the basis of serious issues, a seriousness that was offset by the deepening political disillusionment and apathy of the twenty-first century. But the election of 1970 in Britain did give some plausibility to the communist objection — particularly voiced in Latin America and the 'Third World' — that parliamentary democracy was all very well in Western countries that were so rich that it did not matter which party took office.

Nevertheless, as the years of the early 1970s passed, the Heath government did mark a steady move to the right. The clumsy efforts on the part of the British government in 1988 to prevent the publication of *Spycatcher* by Peter Wright, a senior officer in MI5, the British Secret Service, only served to point out that the book's 'testimony can only be described as convincing', as *The Independent* put it, having bravely published extracts from the work. Wright states that the miners' strike of 1972 and other industrial action 'had a profound effect on the thinking of the Heath Government. Intelligence on domestic subversion became the overriding priority'. Sir Michael Hanley, who had become Director-General of MI5 in 1972, told his officers that Heath wanted 'a major increase in effort' in surveillance of the 'far and wide left' using 'massive technical resources'. Targets included the Workers' Revolutionary Party, the Socialist Workers Party and the Campaign for Nuclear Disarmament (CND).

Wright and other 'old guard, anti-Soviet officers' regarded 'chasing these minor left-wing groupings' as a waste of time. He could also see that while there would be public support for operations against Soviet diplomats, which were naturally seen as operations against the KGB, the public would be uneasy with wholesale surveillance of British citizens. Peter Wright made his own suggestions about killing members of the Provisional IRA by planting booby-trapped detonators on them, justifying the plan on the basis of the violence of the methods of the IRA itself. And in 1988, in the very year that the establishment was attempting to suppress Wright's book, the SAS shot dead three members of an IRA cell in Gibraltar who were unarmed when they were killed. Yet ruthless violence was less corrupting than the pretence that only 'the other side' committed it.[16]

The stupidity of the attitude of Heath's government towards a threat from the Marxist left can be seen rather vividly by looking at Britain in comparison to other European countries, rather than in isolation. Finland's communists enjoyed the support of twenty to twenty-five per cent of the electorate after 1945 and through the 1950s, 1960s and into the 1970s, beyond even the strength of the Italian or French Communist Parties. There was also the fact that Finland had the longest land border with the Soviet Union of any Western European country. Yet nothing demonstrates more clearly than the Finnish situation that a left-wing takeover is possible only through massive public and electoral support (as in Czechoslovakia in 1948) or through military intervention by a foreign power, neither of which were remotely possible in Britain in the 1970s. The label *finlandization* (supine obedience to the Soviet Union) was of course attached to Finland's situation: this was the fate that communists would impose on us, it was said. The reality was not the abstraction *finlandization*, something created by communist influence, but rather the policy of the charismatic, ambitious, authoritarian Finnish President Urho Kekkonen, very much a product of Finland's Western multi-party system, who used Cold War tensions and friendship with the Soviet leaders to strengthen his position.

Edward Heath's outstanding achievement was the successful reopening of negotiations that led to Britain, together with the Irish Republic and Denmark, becoming a member of the European Economic Community, the EEC (later the European Union) on 1 January 1973. However, Heath also moved towards increasingly bitter confrontation with the trade unions through his much hated Industrial Relations Act. Nevertheless, Heath's government continued to act within the limits of post-war consensus politics, and when, in 1973, widespread industrial action including a miners' strike again erupted, industry was put on a three-day week in January 1974. Heath followed this by an appeal to the electorate for support in a general election on 21 February 1974; he failed to win an overall majority or interest the Liberals in a coalition and then resigned, opening the way on 4 March to the return of Wilson as leader of a minority government. A second general election on 10 October of that year gave Labour a small majority. It was the first time that trade union influence led to the defeat of a British government; it was not to happen again.

Almost parallel to these events, the oil crisis that arose from the Israeli-Egyptian-Syrian war in October 1973 brought the post-war boom and the Golden Age to an end in 1974. The Crisis Decades, as Eric Hobsbawm called them, were about to begin, and with them came the watershed in British politics. On 11 February 1975, Heath lost the election for the leadership of the Conservative Party to Margaret Thatcher, who proceeded to tear up the political consensus that had existed since the Second World War, although she did not become Prime Minister until May 1979. Harold Wilson, weary and no doubt afraid that his mental faculties were failing, announced his retirement in the spring of 1976, to be replaced as Labour leader and Prime Minister by James Callaghan on 5 April. Callaghan and his Chancellor of the Exchequer Denis Healey had considerable success, largely forgotten today, in managing and limiting the economic crisis of the 1970s, but this went against the tide of events, which was decisively flowing in the direction of Mrs Thatcher and the newly invigorated right wing of the Conservative Party.

It is useful to pause at this point in the unfolding of post-war events and glance at the world situation in that strange decade, the 1970s. In the East, the Soviet Union was in a state of authoritarian stagnation, albeit less ferocious and somewhat more stable and prosperous than the Stalin era, although the first small steps towards what became known as The Thaw under Khrushchev had actually been made in the last years of Stalin's lifetime—something not often acknowledged even today. By the late seventies, the USSR had attained what was to be the peak of its power and influence, something which the Cold War propaganda in the West had urged us all to regard with dread.

The peak of Soviet power turned out to be something less than apocalyptic; Russian success was exemplified by the

European Security Conference held in Helsinki in summer 1975. It was here that the Soviets got what they had wanted for so long: *recognition of the status quo in Europe*. There were no expansionist Soviet demands to make the West tremble. The conference was also a crowning success for the host country Finland, probably the most left-wing society in Western Europe, as well as the Western country that lived deepest in the Russian shadow. The survival and tenacity of the Finns had been dramatically reflected in the victories of the double gold medallist Lasse Viren in the Olympic Games in Munich in 1972 and Montreal in 1976, restoring the country's pre-Second World War Olympic tradition; with a symbolism that would have seemed strained in a novel or a film, Viren fell heavily halfway through the 10,000 metres race in Munich and then got up to win.

Nevertheless, distrust of the Soviets (and by extension, distrust of those who looked for compromise with them) persisted in Britain, easily fuelled by crude and stupid Russian actions. The dissident writer Alexander Solzhenitsyn was deported from the Soviet Union in February 1974, just a week before the fall of Heath's government in an election brought about by trade union pressure; the British establishment and the popular press found it easy — as ever — to foster a mental association between the Russians abroad and trade unions at home, although the majority of trade union members had as little sympathy as middle England for the Soviet Union, and had less interest in it. Solzhenitsyn had been subjected to appalling pressure for years, although he survived, just as Pasternak had under Khrushchev, after winning the Nobel Prize for *Doctor Zhivago*, just as the majority of prominent Russian writers had survived under Stalin.

Russian tanks were clearly not going to roll down the streets of London; even ill-advised remarks made by Soviet leaders to proudly non-aligned Yugoslavia in 1976 and neutral Finland in 1978 suggesting military cooperation were coldly rebuffed in both cases and not mentioned again. And yet high profile Russian stupidities were more vivid than international realities in the minds of middle class, middlebrow and middle of the road sections of the British public.

What of the world's other superpower in the 1970s? American society continued to be afflicted by the running sore of the Vietnam War. The great American actress Jane Fonda visited North Vietnam, a state with which her country was at war, in July 1972 and talked with Vietnamese citizens, soldiers and political leaders. It must be said that although she was subjected to FBI surveillance and harassment, as well as calls for her trial for treason and a large number of death threats, Jane Fonda would never have been allowed back into her country, or would have served a long prison sentence, if she had been a prominent Soviet citizen who had visited an enemy country.

A ceasefire agreement was finally signed between America and North Vietnam in Paris in 1973, after mutilation, destitution, homelessness or death had befallen millions of Vietnamese (and after large numbers of young Americans had been slaughtered or traumatized) in the previous decade. The final victory of North Vietnam came in April 1975. President Richard Nixon, who had slowly extricated America from Vietnam and also cruelly escalated the bombing of civilians as strategic leverage, resigned on 9 August 1974 over the Watergate scandal: the American presidency was never to be quite the same after this. (As if further settling scores from the sixties, Muhammad Ali regained his heavyweight title just over two months after Nixon's resignation, a title of which he had been stripped because he had refused to be inducted into the US Army to fight in Vietnam. Less well-known are the warm and friendly letters between Ali and the British philosopher and mathematician Bertrand Russell, still campaigning against the Vietnam War and other evils as he approached the age of a hundred.)

However, if democracy in America had been under attack because of Watergate, it was advancing in impoverished Catholic Europe in the seventies. Nearly fifty years of dictatorship in Portugal were brought to an end by a coup of enlightened army officers in 1974; in the following year, the world watched Portugal and feared (or hoped for) a communist takeover, but once again, as in other countries, it did not happen because it lacked the massive support that had existed in Czechoslovakia in 1948; free elections followed in Portugal in the spring of 1976.

British Conservatives had regarded Portugal's right-wing dictators Salazar and, after 1968, Caetano as natural allies. They might have felt equal friendliness towards the Spanish dictator General Franco who died an overdue and prolonged death after a prolonged repressive rule in November 1975, but for Franco's threatening noises over Gibraltar. Spain moved to full parliamentary democracy with impressive decisiveness and swiftness under King Juan Carlos, and together with Portugal was later to join the European Union.

Meanwhile, in pious, conservative and rather backward Catholic Ireland, European membership was the engine of change driving the country forward to the enlightened, prosperous society of the 1990s under the Presidency of Mary Robinson. And in Britain, the first referendum in the country's history, called by Harold Wilson, was held on 5 June 1975 in order to decide upon continued membership of the EEC, with 67.2 per cent of voters in favour; the enthusiasm was not to last.

Reborn German democracy and a rehabilitated Germany were celebrated—by implication—at the Olympic Games in Munich in 1972, together with international sport; the last Olympics to be held in Germany before this had been in Berlin in 1936 with Hitler watching. But the victories of the Finnish runner Lasse Viren, the American swimmer Mark Spitz and the charming Soviet gymnast Olga Korbut were won alongside the horrific events of the seizing of Israeli athletes as hostages by Palestinian guerrillas, the initial killing of two Israelis and the later killing of another nine during a failed German rescue attempt at Munich Airport. It was not to be the last time that the long agony of the Middle East spilt over into the West. Finally, we might say, an uneasy dawn broke one day—probably a day in the year 1974, but certainly in the midst of all these changes—

it was the dawn of the Crisis Decades, the era in which we are still living.

It is necessary to add something else at this point in the account of post-war British history and politics. This chapter and this book generally are concerned with the effect of British politicians upon the society they govern and upon the moral and mental climate of their country. Only the qualities (or lack of them) of these individuals that are relevant to politics and contemporary history are considered. There is nothing to be said here about any politician as a spouse, a parent, a friend or a colleague. The political leaders of large, powerful countries and of many smaller countries are mainly of dubious moral integrity and are habitually deceitful. They typify the moral complexion of the societies in which they rise to power and are tolerated by those societies in varying degrees from country to country. Sadly, political leaders in Britain have steadily declined in both intelligence and integrity since the departures of Attlee and Churchill in 1955. Margaret Thatcher's stature rested on narrow political and administrative skills and great determination; her effect on British society was malignant and destructive and her intellect was astonishingly shallow. The decline of British politics can be seen only too clearly in the array of grey mediocrities, packaged by spin doctors, who lead the political parties today, although it is possible that some as yet untried individuals may reveal abilities that have been overlooked so far.

Margaret Thatcher led the Conservative Party to victory in the election of 3 May 1979, becoming the first woman Prime Minister in British history. And there we come to the first of many illusions, semi-illusions and contradictions. The fact that the new Prime Minister was a woman was of little significance or relevance to the effect she had on British society; her social background and the attitudes that went with it were of immense significance. Mrs Thatcher was always careful to distance herself from feminism and to declare her indifference to it, although the media predictably made a certain amount of fuss about the probability that a woman would take office in the weeks before the election.

The fact of a female Prime Minister probably had psychological importance for a number of her male cabinet colleagues, and that psychological importance may explain the submerged resentment—even hatred—that some of them felt towards her, which would finally surface again at the time of her downfall and removal from office. It had little significance for other women; those women who had strong feminist convictions or at least a keen awareness of the struggle for equality and emancipation were mainly on the political left, disliking Mrs Thatcher as a particularly unpleasant manifestation of British Conservatism. Radical feminists in the seventies and eighties either belonged to the Marxist left or were anarchist-individualist intellectuals who despised governments, with considerable justification, as part of the structure of patriarchal society. (Germaine Greer had written scathingly about the Labour cabinet minister Barbara Castle in *The Female Eunuch* in 1970, long before most people had ever heard of Margaret Thatcher, calling Castle 'the Omnipotent Administrator in frilly knickers'.) Radical and separatist feminists were more common in the 1980s than they are today, at least in some sections of society.

Various community and social work projects proliferated as social inequality and poverty and its consequences increased; such projects also offered short-term and part-time employment, funded by various 'schemes' that grew out of the policies of a government permeated by a visceral loathing of the unemployed and an urgent wish to massage the unemployment figures. There were variations on a joke of the 1980s, and all of them were something like this: 'Co-ordinator needed for community-based advice project. Disabled Black lesbian preferred.' And like most jokes it contained a slice of truth. If there was any connection between Mrs Thatcher's towering presence on the political scene and feminism in the eighties, then it was a strange and oblique one: feminism was strengthened by the sense of anger and social deprivation created by her government because liberation movements are fuelled by injustice. Those who felt or feel any kind of *genuine fondness* for Mrs Thatcher—probably more numerous today because people are nostalgic and sentimental in retrospect—are not usually professional Conservative politicians or among the professional middle class, but rather the lower middle class and the grass-roots Conservative Party membership, as well as some older, non-political working class people. They find a respectable, tough matriarch complete with a handbag full of their own social attitudes very acceptable.

Nevertheless, intelligent people (including women) have sometimes told me that Mrs Thatcher's era has been unduly maligned by left-wing intellectuals—presumably, like myself—after all, she did some good. I sometimes wonder what they mean. Those who have said this are people who lived through the late seventies and the eighties as thinking adults, just as I did. The explanation for this view of the Thatcher era may well lie in the background against which she first came to power. The Labour Prime Minister, James Callaghan, called the early weeks of 1979 'a winter of discontent', and the phrase was picked up by the newspapers and used by the *Daily Telegraph* on 9 February and *The Sun* on 30 April. It was a time of snow and bitter weather, strikes, disputes and what seemed to be an unravelling social infrastructure. It was a long episode that the Left try to ignore, and the Right—and the popular press at the time—exaggerated and still exaggerate. After all, the majority of hospital patients in early 1979 were *not* left without treatment and the majority of British people did *not* encounter unburied corpses stored in overflowing mortuaries or walk between piles of uncollected rubbish on the streets. However, behind this discontent a deeper discontent had emerged.

The industrial and social disruption was not in itself decisive; similar experiences only five years before had led the electorate to reject a Conservative government and vote in Labour. The truth is that there was a deep dislike and resentment smouldering in a considerable number of people and it was directed at the Labour government, the Labour Party, Labour controlled local councils and the trade union leadership and bureaucracy. The Marxist historian Eric Hobsbawm—who, as we have seen, is still regarded as a target worth swiping at by the *Daily Mail* even today—pointed out in 1978 in a published lecture that trade unions pursued the narrow economic interest of one group of workers 'irrespective of the rest', relying on 'inconvenience they might cause to the public' and so 'increased potential friction between groups of workers'.[17, 18] Thus, matters had reached the point at which even trade union members could dislike trade union power in general. To this I might add the far from minor fact that Labour councils sent carpenters or plumbers who turned up on the doorsteps of the tenants of council houses to replace perfectly good doors with inferior doors or to make other unwanted and inexplicable changes to the homes of hardworking people, some of whom were skilled or semi-skilled workers who naturally wanted to own a house and be free of this interference.

Margaret Thatcher appealed to these people. Of course, her government did little or nothing to prevent such interference in the lives of individuals and the reality of buying their own homes was a huge disappointment for many people. The fact remains: the leadership and bureaucracy of the Labour Party and the trade unions at national and local level in 1979 frequently *were* authoritarian, complacent and smug with power. The feeling that Mrs Thatcher was prepared to cut through the layers of a suffocating, inert mass that was clogging society—and today the memory of that feeling—do much to explain the assertion that 'after all, she did some good'.

The phrase 'winter of discontent' is a misquotation of the opening lines of Shakespeare's *Richard III*: 'Now is the winter of our discontent / Made glorious summer by this sun of York.' Quite often, only the first seven words are quoted. The sense of the passage, which is that winter is over and summer has arrived, as well as the vicious irony with which Gloucester is speaking, are often overlooked—he is, he tells us, 'rudely stamp'd... deform'd, unfinish'd', he is not fitted for 'this weak piping time of peace'. Gloucester misses having 'fearful adversaries', or as Mrs Thatcher would put it, 'the enemy without' (Argentines), while 'Here the enemy is within' (miners).

If Callaghan had possessed the literary sophistication of Churchill or Aneurin Bevan he might have quoted more accurately or not quoted this passage at all. But perhaps Callaghan and Mrs Thatcher's supporters in the press who picked up his words were unwittingly prophetic. The new Prime Minister, the most divisive, aggressive and confrontational British leader of the twentieth century, quoted St Francis of Assisi on the steps of 10 Downing Street in May 1979: 'Where there is discord, may we bring harmony. Where there is error, may we bring truth. Where there is doubt, may we bring faith. Where there is despair, may we bring hope.' Did her speech writers or Gordon Reece, the ex-television producer who fashioned her public image, or Mrs Thatcher herself — perhaps it really was a favourite quotation of hers — appreciate the irony, particularly as the years passed?

Individuals seem always to remain the same even after becoming leaders with immense power. They continue to be what they were before attaining power and they act and react accordingly. Churchill was a maverick aristocrat adventurer steeped in literature and learning. Stalin was a revolutionary bandit-conspirator of high intelligence and wide reading. Hitler was a psychopathic drifter, semi-educated and carried away by banal racist notions, but possessing an extraordinary grasp of political and military strategy. Margaret Thatcher was the daughter of a fundamentalist Christian grocer and town councillor, and she inherited the visceral hatred of trade unions and socialism that her father shared with those who came from that social background. Her iron determination and self-discipline, her lack of breadth of culture and her narrow intelligence can be understood in terms of her upbringing and early life; if she had been more intelligent she would have distanced herself from her father's view of the world because she would have possessed a more complex understanding of life, instead she never ceased to identify with her father's values.

It is instructive to recall that Churchill wrote a description of Lenin in *The Aftermath*, a sequel to *The World Crisis*, his history of the First World War. This description is fundamentally hostile and sometimes inaccurate, at least by implication. However, Churchill catches a good deal of the essence of Lenin as a personality and a figure in world history, just as an idiosyncratic painting can catch the essence of a human face. Possibly, Aneurin Bevan or even Michael Foot could have written something of the same quality. Mrs Thatcher, despite her confident pronouncements on Marxism—of which she was almost completely ignorant—would have been incapable of writing something like this because she simply lacked sufficient understanding of the world. (Tony Blair, Thatcher's true heir and spiritual/political successor, a similarly uncultured politician, would have done no better.)

Her intellectual level is amply indicated by the following comment on the miners' strike: 'What the strike's defeat established was that Britain could not be made ungovernable by the Fascist Left. Marxists wanted to defy the law of the land in order to defy the laws of economics.'[19] 'Marxist Left' was no doubt too mild and neutral for her purposes, and 'extreme Left' would not quite do either (possibly she was mindful of how often she had been called a representative of the extreme Right), and 'authoritarian Left' would hardly be a suitable term of abuse from the pen of this apostle of Victorian values. 'Fascist Marxists' or 'Fascist socialists' would have been too grotesque even for the Iron Lady. But the concoction 'Fascist Left' expressed everything she hated in a handy, concentrated form.

It is quite unnecessary to come down to Mrs Thatcher's level of silliness by calling her a fascist, as her opponents sometimes very stupidly did. Naturally, she was not a fascist. And yet there are some illuminating and suggestive parallels to be drawn. In a review of a translation of *Mein Kampf* in 1940 Orwell said of Hitler, 'a thing that strikes one is the rigidity of his mind, the way in which his world-view *doesn't* develop'. The same was true of Margaret Thatcher; her utterances in the 1990s were astonishingly similar to her utterances in the 1970s. Secondly, she shared with fascism the conviction that war is a valid means of restoring national glory: 'We have ceased to be a nation in retreat. We have instead a newfound confidence—born in the economic battles at home and tested and found true eight thousand miles away...' (Speech on the 'Falklands Spirit', Cheltenham, 3 July 1982). Thirdly, Margaret Thatcher was—like Hitler—conducting a thoroughgoing revolution in national life, aimed at the old, entrenched ruling class and its methods as well as at the labour movement; and because of left-wing confusion and weakness that revolution was able to command just enough electoral support for over a decade. Finally, despite preaching the notion of rolling back the power of the state, Mrs Thatcher concentrated vast centralized power in her hands; there had been warnings that Britain was becoming more of an 'elective dictatorship' than almost any other Western country well before 1979; after 1979 the force of the 'elective dictatorship' greatly increased—it has not diminished since the 1980s.

Personally, with adult memories of Britain before 1979, I find it difficult as a parent to convey fully to my daughter Emma Anne, a PhD researcher who has memories only of post-Thatcher Britain, the depth and scale of the changes in British society, many of which have turned out to be permanent and irreversible. I hope that what I have written in this chapter has conveyed that Britain before Margaret Thatcher was very far from being an entirely free, democratic and fair society. Britain after Mrs Thatcher has been radically different and considerably worse and has not shown any sign yet that it can escape from the mould she imposed upon it.

The seemingly inexorable Thatcher revolution marched onwards. Today, perhaps, it is easier to see that it was not so inexorable and certainly not inevitable. Margaret Thatcher called herself a handbag economist; she was indeed a handbag economist and politician and a handbag actor in world affairs and commentator upon them—her thinking never rose above that level. Her revolution, like all revolutions, was driven by an idea: you run the affairs of a country (it is not appropriate to say 'society', the existence of which she denied) like a business, according to the instincts of businessmen and businesswomen. People in all areas of life, teachers within the education system, including the universities, doctors within the Health Service, were urged to think competitively, to apply sound business sense; many of them began to do so and have continued in this way. Although Mrs Thatcher lacked any understanding of the Marxism she hated, Karl Marx had given an enduring description of the *spirit* of her revolution in *The Communist Manifesto*, almost a century and a half earlier:

> [Capitalism] has left remaining no other nexus between man and man than naked self-interest, than callous 'cash payment'. It has drowned the most heavenly ecstasies of religious fervour, of chivalrous enthusiasm, of philistine sentimentalism, in the icy water of egotistical calculation. It has resolved personal worth into exchange value... In one word, for exploitation, veiled by religious and political illusions, it has substituted naked, shameless, direct, brutal exploitation.

Sadly, the fragmented literature of the eighties, fiction, non-fiction, political writing, poetry and drama (despite the interesting and impressive efforts of Caryl Churchill), never gave us anything that possessed Marx's precision, poise and passion. Aside from this, the self-evident fact that business aspirations and the business approach to the world have limits that should be set by common decency was accepted by all parties from 1945 until the mid-seventies — it had taken long enough to make even that advance.

The claim that Mrs Thatcher reduced larger numbers of people to poverty and made larger numbers of the rich richer still in a shorter space of time than any other post-war leader looks like a cliché, a rhetorical flourish. Unfortunately, it happens to be a fact documented by the UN: substantial poverty increased in Britain from the early 1980s to 1997 more quickly than in any other country, with 'income poverty' increasing by almost sixty per cent under the Thatcher government.[20] 'You cannot hide the poorest behind national boundaries', another UN report reminded us, writing of the class war being waged in the world. National boundaries were, of course, at the heart of the Thatcher view of the world and are deeply imbedded in British attitudes, so that the UN has frequently irritated British governments; in 2013 the popular press once again reacted with venom when a UN official presumed to comment on the human cost of economic and financial policies in Britain.

About a quarter of British adults were living in poverty by 1996, double the number of people in that condition in 1979, the year that Mrs Thatcher came to power, with one child in three born into poverty in Britain by the same year, making British society — together with Australian society — the most unequal in the Western world.[21, 22, 23] The march of the facts is undeniable and far more inexorable than Mrs Thatcher's own march ever need have been; the reality tends to be rather brutal in trampling on the silliness, illusions and lies of the handbag revolution — vulgar even by the standards of political posturing — many of them still promoted by New Labour and more recently by the Coalition ('a new government and a new kind of government').

The real course that events took is breathtakingly simple: a contradiction of one of the most basic justifications of capitalism. Wealth did not gradually move downwards from above; it swiftly shifted upwards from below. In the period 1979 to 1993 the real income, after housing costs, of the poorest tenth of British society fell by eighteen per cent, while the richest tenth of the population saw their income rise by sixty-one per cent. The post-war transformation of life in the so-called Golden Age was simply reversed. No one disagreed with Mrs Thatcher about the way in which the economy had ceased to function well since the beginning of the 1970s. And yet her policies did not address that problem, but instead shifted huge amounts of available wealth to those who were already well off.[24, 25]

The bitterest irony — or perhaps the most farcical illusion and the most cynical deception — lay in the fact that the policies pursued by a Prime Minister who embraced Victorian values undermined family life. In a time when child benefit was frozen, unemployment rose to two million and then to three million, home ownership was promoted together with hostility to providing council housing, and spending on education was cut, the strain on the finances of families made them less self-reliant, so that 'Many families and individuals have had their ability to care for themselves reduced, not increased', as Pamela Abbott and Claire Wallace wrote, concluding, 'The welfare and economic policies advocated by the New Right... have been more concerned with reasserting the rights of middle class men and maintaining capitalism than they have been with a genuine concern for men, women and children and the quality of their lives'.[26]

These facts speak for themselves, disclosing the real changes in Britain behind the Thatcherite claims of the eighties and the haze through which that revolution is sometimes seen today. The handbag revolution did not, of course, involve the savagery, loss of life and sheer scale of another revolution faraway and long ago, carried out for very different motives. And yet the verdict of Eric Hobsbawm on Stalin's revolution is eerily applicable to the true effect of Thatcherism on life in Britain, it is 'shameful and beyond palliation, let alone justification'.

Two years into Mrs Thatcher's first term of office her revolution seemed to be faltering and there was serious doubt that she could win another election. The Thatcher enterprise was obligingly saved by Argentina in the following year. The Argentines invaded the British dependency of the Falkland Islands, population 1,800, on 2 April 1982. The fates were extremely kind to Mrs Thatcher, who maintained in her memoirs that the war was quite unexpected.

Or was it? There had been failed diplomatic negotiations over sovereignty in New York in February; a low key infiltration of one of the islands, South Georgia, was carried out by the Argentines; Britain had one of the most powerful intelligence services in the world; Argentina was ruled by a crude military junta and was hardly a model of efficiency—utterly different from disciplined and perpetually besieged communist Cuba. And yet the British government chose to leave the islands undefended against the ramshackle Argentine army that mainly consisted of ill-equipped conscripts, seeming to be unable to foresee something so likely—in those circumstances—as military action by Argentina. However, robust preventative measures would not have suited an unpopular Prime Minister, with power slipping from her grasp, nearly so well as the war that followed. Was the war allowed to happen by tacit invitation and a convincing display of near indifference to the fate of the islands? No convincing proof of this has yet been found and historians will continue to argue over the matter. Argentina naturally presented no threat whatsoever to Britain itself, but Mrs Thatcher was able to act as if it did and play the great war leader at the cost of only a thousand lives (a small price, except for the families—British and Argentine—of those killed, or for the servicemen permanently mutilated by wounds); it would indeed have taken a Prime Minister of military genius to contrive defeat at the hands of Argentina.

All non-military solutions were brushed aside, just as preventative measures had not been taken: a blockade without direct military engagement, economic sanctions against Argentina in which many countries would have readily participated, diplomatic pressure—which would have been willingly exerted—by the USA, and an offer of mediation by Peru. The war appealed to the worst attitudes of the British, including the sense of inferiority that had lingered since Suez and feelings of the kind that so often lead to the perception of the England team playing football against a European side as heroes doing battle against our enemies while treacherous politicians sell out our interests. (Later, even Blair in run-of-the-mill negotiations with other members of the European Union was sometimes portrayed as a spineless quisling; Mrs Thatcher, by conviction and political shrewdness, always presented herself as Britain's defender against the Europeans.)

The war also prepared the way for the eventual destruction of the mining industry and the National Union of Mineworkers, and for a comment on the miners by Mrs Thatcher, which was —even for her—unusual in its viciousness and sheer irresponsibility. 'In the Falklands we had to fight the enemy without. Here the enemy is within and it is much more difficult to fight, but just as dangerous to liberty' (Speech to the 1922 Committee, July 1984).

Arthur Scargill, president of the NUM, called a national strike in March 1984 over the decision by the National Coal Board to close what it defined as 'uneconomic pits'. He predicted that this was the first stage of the dismantling and destruction of the mining industry, and although his claim was ridiculed again and again by the media it was precise and accurate, as even books sympathetic to Mrs Thatcher later described. About 200,000 people were employed in the mining industry in 1985, but in 1995 there were only 11,000; pit after pit was closed; thriving mining communities lost the reason for their existence and sank into ghost town conditions of mass unemployment, dwindling economic activity, closed down shops and businesses and a large-scale exodus of local people; entire vibrant areas of population were destroyed.[27]

The NUM was also destroyed as a political, social and industrial force and the trade union movement was weakened beyond recognition. The attack on the miners and on Scargill by the popular tabloid press reached depths of fabrication, venom, stupidity and sheer craziness unparalleled in a Western democracy in the post-war era; otherwise responsible journalists on newspapers of usually unchallengeable integrity often joined in the chorus of hate and hysteria directed at Scargill. *The Sun* doctored a photograph to make Arthur Scargill look like Hitler, but it was the tabloid campaign that was so strongly reminiscent of Nazism. Lamentably, *The Observer*, *New Statesman*, *The Independent* and even at one point, amazingly (given the pioneering efforts of one of its journalists), *The Guardian* also routinely attacked the miners' leader. In March 1990, long after the strike and the defeat of the miners, the *Daily Mirror* published a story accusing Scargill of using money from Colonel Gaddafi of Libya, intended to finance the strike, to pay his mortgage; subsequently, he was also accused of embezzling millions of pounds in donations from Soviet miners. One of the sources for these allegations was Roger Windsor, a former NUM official, subsequently identified in Parliament as an MI5 agent. A full inquiry was carried out by Gavin Lightman, QC, later a judge in the High Court, finding the allegations made by Roger Windsor against Scargill 'entirely untrue'. Apart from claims by Windsor and other intelligence sources who were not even named, for which no proof was ever offered, there is no evidence that the NUM was ever given money by Gaddafi. However, this story is sometimes repeated in print even today. Windsor tried to sue Scargill, but withdrew his actions for libel and was ordered to pay costs; the Inland Revenue found Scargill and the NUM innocent of the misdirection of funds; the Fraud Squad abandoned its own investigation. The investigative *Guardian* journalist Seumas Milne documented the MI5 campaign against Scargill and the miners, which had been ordered by Margaret Thatcher, in his book *The Enemy Within*, proving his case beyond any reasonable doubt. Overworked words such as 'chilling' and 'terrifying' really do apply to Milne's book.[28]

Or perhaps we should not be so very shocked in the light of Peter Wright's book, *Spycatcher* (1987). Wright records that in 1974 about thirty of his fellow MI5 officers were planning to leak files that would suggest that Harold Wilson was a security risk and possibly a Soviet agent; Wright was only dissuaded from joining them, and giving assistance crucial to the plan, by his friend Victor Rothschild, appointed by Edward Heath in 1970 as head of the Central Policy Review Staff (CPRS) — the Think Tank. And after 11 September 2001, the War on Terror, post-liberal social control, the electronic tagging of suspected terrorists who are not charged, put on trial or even informed of the reasons for the actions taken against them, MI5 has become more active and powerful than ever. Gerry Adams of Sinn Fein, in an interview in 2009, claimed that:

> There are people in the intelligence services who would know that the sensible way forward is politically. But there's another tendency... I remember one meeting we had during negotiations with the British government... [In] the other room [t]here was a sizeable group — five or six men — in plain clothes... a senior Irish Government official said, 'That's the nub of the

problem, Gerry. Because they're the spooks, and they haven't given up.'

Johann Hari, the interviewer, who also wrote a long background article on Gerry Adams, wonders: 'Can this be true? Where's the evidence?' However, if we set this claim alongside other, well-documented examples of the activities of MI5 and the British establishment, it takes on a different light.[29]

Gerry Adams was arrested and questioned for four days at the beginning of May 2014, and then released without charge. The police were investigating claims made by two individuals, both now dead, that Mr Adams was involved in the murder of Jean McConville by the IRA in 1972 — these allegations had been made while participating in an 'oral history' of the Northern Ireland conflict assembled by Boston College. Significantly, Gerry Adams and the leadership of Sinn Fein insisted that a 'cabal', 'the dark side' or the 'old guard' in the Police Service of Northern Ireland wanted to damage the peace process. Those participating in the oral history project had been assured that their statements would not be made public until after their deaths. Only an application by the PSNI and a ruling by an American court made the tapes available to the police. The release of Gerry Adams without charge and the circumstances in which the allegations were originally made and then later used by the police all seem to give great weight to his references in 2009 and 2014 to 'another tendency' in the police and intelligence services.

In *The Gulag Archipelago*, Solzhenitsyn calls the Soviet State Security Service 'that flexible, unitary organism inhabiting a nation as a tapeworm inhabits a human body'. Just what should we say about the British secret intelligence service?

Could the Miners' Strike of 1984–85 have turned out differently? The answer is surely yes. Only a little more support and solidarity from other trade unions would have led to a victory for the miners. Explicit support from Neil Kinnock, leader of the Labour Party, would have made a considerable difference. Mrs Thatcher challenged Kinnock with scathing contempt in Parliament for remaining silent and not *attacking* the NUM; his silence was indeed contemptible, but for the opposite reason. If the miners had won, the role and position of the unions would have changed even more, with consequences for the complexion of the Labour Party also (no doubt this was one of Kinnock's considerations).

Margaret Thatcher's government could not have won a general election in the aftermath of a miners' victory, or remained in office without military intervention, martial law and some kind of state of emergency. Rejection of Thatcherism and a reinvigorated labour movement would have generated social change amounting to the beginnings of revolution. In a worldwide recession such upheavals in Britain would have had an enormous impact on the working class in other European states. None of this can be lightly dismissed as fantasy. As Terry Eagleton points out in *Why Marx Was Right* (2011), 'if you do not resist the apparently inevitable, you will never know how inevitable the inevitable was'.

The problem lay in the weakness and indeed the lack of viability of the opposition and in the dismal fortunes of the Labour Party. Michael Foot was elected leader of the Party in 1980 — a cultured intellectual of great integrity and a fine, old-fashioned orator, but impossible to imagine as Prime Minister. The electorate did not imagine it and the general election of summer 1983 returned the Conservatives with a crushing majority of 144 seats. In 1981, Tony Benn was narrowly defeated by Denis Healey in the contest for the Labour deputy leadership. Neil Kinnock replaced Foot in 1983 after the near-terminal election disaster, proceeding to expel the Trotskyite Militant Tendency from the Party and completing the process of ending the hopes and ambitions of the Marxist left, which had begun with Benn's defeat in 1981. Some leading Labour figures quit the Party in 1981 to form the Social Democratic Party: that vapid political grouping, an expression of well-meaning middle class wishful thinking, captured enough votes, together with the Liberals, to seriously worry Labour and to a lesser extent Mrs Thatcher also.

The hollowness of the Social Democrats gradually became apparent to the electorate, so that they merged and sank without trace in the Liberal Party, leaving only the awkward name Liberal Democrats as evidence of their passing. Possibly some remnant of their influence has made the moral and political compromises of the Liberals in coalition with Cameron's Conservatives easier and more acceptable. Ask an intelligent A-Level student today to tell you about the Social Democrats of the eighties and she is likely to answer you with a blank look, unless she has a particular passion for political history.

I cannot agree with Eric Hobsbawm that Kinnock expressed and was motivated by the determination of the non-Bennite Labour left to save the Party from the wildly unrealistic Trotskyites. Kinnock exhibited a self-serving opportunism that was unusually crass even among politicians, as his astute and timely resignation from the Campaign for Nuclear Disarmament (CND) demonstrates. Ultimately, Kinnock's hollowness — like that of the Social Democrats — became apparent.

The narrow defeat of Labour under Kinnock in the 1992 election *was* a tragedy for the Labour Party, the labour movement and for Britain, not because of the virtues of Labour, but because of the triumph of something worse. The failure and the responsibility for failure were largely Kinnock's. There was no prospect of a Labour government after 1992, only the increasing certainty of government by Blair's 'New Labour'; the Labour Party itself rapidly ceased to exist when Blair became leader. The British Labour Party may never have amounted to very much, but in the context of capitalist multi-party democracy its disappearance was a desolating blow to the society out of which it had grown.

I recall seeing Neil Kinnock in Swansea in the mid-1980s at a function of the Welsh NUM, sitting beside the union leadership. When one of the miners' leaders rose to give an introductory speech, he was interrupted by an expert heckler. The Welsh-English affirmative *aye* is spoken with a very long 'a', not the short 'a' of the English 'aye'. It can convey fondness, enthusiasm, agreement or derision and sarcasm. The miners' leader spoke of the recent national strike of 1984–85: 'Unfortunately, some people allowed us to remain isolated.' Then the heckler cried out: 'Aye! There's one of the buggers sitting there by you!' I also recall Kinnock giving a speech before the national strike ended, saying something like: 'I condemn violence, I oppose violence, I abominate violence, I do not tolerate violence.' He then made a slight, but unfortunate, pause and a heckler shouted wearily: 'What's your position on violence then, Neil?' It is a pity that working class wit and the wisdom contained in it are not present more often. Like many other good things in British culture, they are increasingly hard to find. The traditional British values out of which Orwell hoped a non-communist socialist revolution would grow in 1941 have largely ceased to exist. Extraordinary *events* and upheavals can happen in many different societies, but a revolution is a process not an event.

Mrs Thatcher herself was a victim of the casting away of norms and standards in political life that had endured since 1945. She was effectively removed from office by her own colleagues in November 1990. The convulsions she had brought about in the life of the country had been so thoroughgoing and successful that the spectacle of her downfall did not seem all that strange. And yet here was a serving Prime Minister who had won three general elections; her party had a reduced but still huge majority since the election of 1987; the first war on Iraq by America, into which Britain would inevitably and obediently be drawn within months, was just the kind of event that would boost her popularity; although many of her policies were hated and her party was sliding in the opinion polls, she had survived that before.

Geoffrey Howe, who had served as both Chancellor of the Exchequer and Foreign Secretary, resigned from the cabinet. Howe's approach to Europe (and the approach of other ministers who turned on her) did not in the long run turn out to be much different from Mrs Thatcher's approach—certainly nothing like the real gulf that separated her attitude to Europe from that of Edward Heath. Howe delivered a devastating attack on Mrs Thatcher in the House of Commons on 13 November 1990, likened by some commentators to Leo Amery's words to Chamberlain in 1940: 'In the name of God, go.' She was opposed in the Conservative Party leadership election later that month, winning a clear majority of votes but not enough to avoid a second ballot. Mrs Thatcher at first announced that she would stand in the second ballot. But in private conversations her cabinet told her, one by one, that they did not think she could win, or at least not win convincingly—or did they tell her explicitly or by implication that they would not serve under her? It amounted to the same thing: Margaret Thatcher withdrew from the contest and resigned.

Her own description of Howe's speech was probably accurate, 'this final act of bile and treachery'; it applied to most of those around her. Could she have gambled boldly and survived, calling a snap general election as soon as Howe's speech made it inevitable that she would be opposed in the leadership contest, ensuring that even if she was removed as party leader, her successor could never consolidate his position and win the general election? Politicians being what they are, she might have found herself unopposed after all. There were still many admirers of her ruthlessness in the parliamentary party and many more in the grassroots party (and there are still many at that level to this day), so that such determination and defiance might have succeeded.

When it came to the decisive moment, however, she caved in. (It is instructive to reflect that Margaret Thatcher could not have foreseen the IRA bombing of the hotel in Brighton at which she and several of her ministers were staying in October 1984; she took no *conscious* risks, exhibited no personal bravery and was certainly well guarded.) In fact, there have been very, very few British politicians since the 1970s, in government or opposition, who have ever faced any personal risk or danger to themselves—like Mrs Thatcher they have sometimes led hardworking lives, but have been sheltered and privileged, imposing hardship and desperation on others, ordering British servicemen to their deaths and taking the lives of the citizens of other countries, but doing so from the safety of an office or committee room.

This applies most of all, of course, to Tony Blair, who sent British forces into action five times in six years. It was said that Margaret Thatcher had become increasingly autocratic in style and detached from reality. Was she more detached from reality than the Prime Minister who led Britain into war with talk of Weapons of Mass Destruction that later could not be found, in obedience to an American President who wanted 'regime change', in defiance of a demonstration by two million of his fellow UK citizens, without allowing UN weapons inspectors time to complete their work because they were disproving his claims?

John Major was elected leader of the Conservatives in place of Mrs Thatcher, presiding over the first British war against Iraq in 1991, in obedience—so to speak—to the first Bush. There was a good deal of idle speculation about Major representing a return to the politics of the centre, distancing himself from Thatcher as he abandoned the deeply hated poll tax. Things did not improve very rapidly even in this respect. My partner was sent to prison in November 1992 for refusing to pay the poll tax on moral grounds, ironically during one of the short periods we spent in Britain between 1991 and 1993, having returned from Spain where we lived for most of that time—a period to which I shall return in the Afterword to this book. I vividly remember visiting her in a women's prison outside Bristol with our daughter, then aged three. I was narrowly overlooked and avoided imprisonment because of the frequent changes in our working lives and our spells abroad: I certainly would not have paid the tax.

When in Britain we lived in Swansea at that time. Apart from my partner, I recall that the only other Swansea resident to be imprisoned for non-payment was a young man with learning difficulties; a week or so before his imprisonment he had pursued a mugger who had snatched a woman's handbag in the centre of Swansea and got the bag back for her. Orwell had said it in his essay *Raffles and Miss Blandish* in 1944: 'Perhaps the basic myth of the Western world is Jack the Giant-killer, but to be brought up to date this should be renamed Jack the Dwarf-killer.' It is hardly stretching the point to observe that the British have allowed politicians like Eden in Suez, Wilson in his treatment of the Chagossians, Thatcher in the coalmining areas and in the Falklands, Major and Blair in Iraq and Afghanistan and in the detention centres for terrorists held without charge, trial or conviction, to redefine their country, their society and themselves in just such a way.

How profoundly the country that faced Hitler in 1940 has changed! The Conservatives under John Major defeated Labour in the 1992 election; five months later there came 'Black Wednesday', the financial crisis that took Britain out of the European Exchange Rate Mechanism. Major lost much of his underserved reputation for unusual honesty by equivocating about his own share of responsibility in the matter. The lesson that could never be acknowledged—repeated in 2008—was that global capitalism as a system does not work and cannot avoid such upheavals. But an appeal for a return to basic values must have seemed good material for tabloid headlines and a good diversionary tactic to Major; when this overlapped with sleaze, dishonesty and scandals in political life, the public came to regard him with outright dislike. Continued Conservative rule was no longer viable or tenable. Tony Blair led the party that he and others (not least Mrs Thatcher, indirectly) had constructed in place of the Labour Party to a spectacular election victory in May 1997, winning an extraordinary majority of 179 seats.

An account of the moral and political atmosphere in Britain and its nearest neighbours should include some consideration of the impact of women in public life. The historians Eric Hobsbawm and Alan Palmer are both careful to do this; and it is an area in which we find both grounds for hope and cause for disappointment. There were women in Britain and beyond in 1997 whose feminine qualities had an impact of infinitely greater importance than the fact that Mrs Thatcher had happened to be Britain's first woman Prime Minister. The word 'feminine' itself had returned from its opprobrium and exile by feminists in the 1980s. Mary Robinson was elected President of Ireland in 1990, the year of Margaret Thatcher's downfall, and served until 1997 when she became UN High Commissioner for Human Rights. Diana the Princess of Wales was campaigning against land mines in Africa in early 1997, attracting venomous and patronizing attacks from certain MPs and ministers, including Peter Viggers and Earl Howe; yet her death in August of that year caused an amazing outpouring of collective grief. Also in 1997, the first of the *Harry Potter* books was published, but few would then have predicted or even imagined the later literary development of J.K. Rowling — something that we must consider at length further on. In 2014, one of the few politicians who gave the impression that the Labour Party still tenuously lives on is Stella Creasy, MP for Walthamstow — this impression may of course be mistaken; there is a long list of once inspiring women Labour MPs who failed to live up to expectations, from Shirley Williams (later of the Social Democratic Party) to Clare Short, who delayed a principled resignation over the Iraq war until she had lost credibility. Nevertheless, Jack the Dwarf-killer has not entirely prevailed after all — Jackie the Giant-killer still walks the land.

John Smith, who led the Labour Party after Kinnock and before Blair, died suddenly in May 1994; it was the end of the life and career of a man who possessed unusual decency for a professional politician, seeming to be moved by real feelings of indignation over injustice. Whether Smith would have been elected Prime Minister and what sort of government he would have headed are questions that can never be answered. Death is unanswerable — the fact that we so often forget, namely that what happens in history is not inevitable, does not apply here. John Smith died and did not become Prime Minister; Blair did not die and was elected to lead Britain.

It is unlikely that Smith would have led what would have been regarded as a Labour government until 1992, indeed he was part of the process of consigning the Labour Party to the past, although he did not play that part with anything like Blair's thoroughness and completeness. It is also unlikely that he would have shown Blair's disturbing subservience to the Americans—although this is far from certain. As well as the wars in which Blair embroiled Britain, it is important to recognize that he accepted 'too much of the ideological assumptions of the prevailing free market economic theology. Not least the assumption which destroys the foundations of all movements for improving the condition of the people [and of] Labour governments, namely that the efficient conduct of a society's affairs can only be by the search for personal advantage, i.e. by behaving like businessmen' (Eric Hobsbawm, *Interesting Times*, 2002). The facts show that Hobsbawm puts it rather mildly.

Blair and his strategists went much further than Kinnock, whose opportunism and failures had started to bring the Labour Party tumbling down. Before winning the 1997 election, Peter Mandelson and Roger Liddle had written of the arms industry and 'the pre-eminence of the City of London' as strengths and virtues in the British economy.[30] The pivotal act was carried out very early on. Chancellor Gordon Brown's first budget gave the financiers of the Bank of England, elected by no one, the power to fix interest rates, thus relinquishing a vital method of intervening in the economy needed by *any government* of any party, something that was unthinkable until before the mid-1990s. The *Financial Times* of 23 June 1997 recognized some of the long-term social implications of New Labour's policy. Blair's government also abolished universal free tuition and replaced student grants with loans, going further than Mrs Thatcher had ever done. The reality quickly became apparent to anyone who cared to look. Even within the context of Western capitalist multi-party systems, Britain became (and still is) a one party state based on a single ideology of the free market; party names became names only, and genuine political and electoral choice—even to the extent that it had existed from 1945 to 1997—simply evaporated.

One piece of political dishonesty and deceit has become increasingly important since Blair first came to power. British politicians had been obsessed by the number of unemployed since the near full employment of the Golden Age had begun to crumble in the early seventies, calling up memories of the 1930s. More and more ingenious methods of massaging the unemployment figures were invented. Temporary, part-time, short-term and irregular forms of employment have become more and more useful and significant for politicians since 1997; misleading and carefully managed totals of those without a job are used to cover up a number of facts, and most of all to conceal the actual circumstances of large numbers of ordinary families. For instance, the unemployed plumber, electrician, taxi driver, caterer or hairdresser who signs on as unemployed and manages to make ends meet by doing cash-in-hand work *as well as* drawing Jobseekers' Allowance is usually no better off by becoming 'self-employed' and claiming Working Tax Credit. He or she is mainly worse off because some of the other benefits that go with Jobseekers' Allowance are reduced or no longer available. Housing Benefit for those in council or housing association homes or other rented accommodation usually goes down for the 'self-employed'. The same applies to those who have been unable to work due to illness and then manage to go on getting medical certificates from a friendly doctor and quietly do cash-in-hand work. When they become 'self-employed' and no longer receive what is now Employment and Support Allowance, the benefit now paid to those who are too ill to work, they lose other small but extremely important entitlements. It was made easy to get Working Tax Credit as a self-employed person; low earnings are rarely checked and are easy not to declare, and have to be quite substantial before Working Tax Credit is affected. Large numbers of people go on doing much the same work—sometimes very infrequent—and are often worse off than when they are officially unemployed. From another direction, especially since the Conservative-Liberal coalition came to power in 2010, benefits for those who are genuinely and severely ill have been attacked; there has been the hideous spectacle of very sick and disabled people being told that they are capable of part-time work and 'light duties'.

How much the 'improved unemployment figures' and 'falling numbers of those who have no job' actually convince sensible members of the public is difficult to judge. The popular press never ceases in its attempts to persuade people who are struggling to pay their bills that someone else is having a good time at their expense—benefit cheats, the work-shy, asylum seekers and at present immigrants from Europe. Of course, the dynamics of capitalism mean that someone else *is* having a good time at the expense of deprived and impoverished people because the system needs large numbers of people—whether in advanced capitalist countries or elsewhere—to live in various degrees of poverty in order to function. Large sections of society or entire national populations may grow very prosperous indeed, but somewhere else other people must get poorer and often fall into destitution. This is such an inevitable consequence of the capitalist system that it could not be prevented by every banker, millionaire, chief executive of a large company and owner of a media or manufacturing empire in the world undergoing a change of heart like that of Scrooge.

In Britain since 1979, however, the political leaders who have administered the system—Margaret Thatcher, John Major, Tony Blair, Gordon Brown and David Cameron—have acted with a brutality and cheerful lack of moral restraint that is breathtaking. The reality, of course, is more complicated than some simple-minded opponents of capitalism will admit. Outside the small neo-Nazi groups, no British politician can think— let alone act—as a South American military dictator would think and act. All five of the leaders I have just named, and especially Blair, Major and Cameron, have believed in some genuine human values with a part of their minds for most of the time. Major and Cameron particularly have sometimes acted on humane impulses and tried to bring about enlightened changes. There is no reason to suppose that Major is simply being untruthful when he says that he wishes that fewer of the positions of power in Britain were filled by men from a privileged elite. The fact that he has spent his life upholding a system that perpetuates that situation, which cannot be changed by this or that specific decision, is an insight that he cannot permit himself.

For mainstream British politicians there is a point at which intellectual honesty and self-awareness must be replaced by a strenuous act of self-deception. After that point, only three things can happen: the self-deception is maintained or the individual becomes an outright cynical villain or the individual leaves political life. No doubt something similar applies to most American political leaders also. Furthermore, a simplistic, two-dimensional philosophy of life, general ignorance and shallowness of intellect made self-deception easier for Margaret Thatcher and Tony Blair — and, of course, for President George W. Bush. (Notably, even a film director of the stature of Oliver Stone quite failed to make Bush interesting; unlike his superb and moving film about Nixon, Stone's *W.*, his cinematic biography of Bush, is merely as boring as its subject.) We can only wonder if it is too charitable to ascribe self-deception and ignorance to the inspiring example set by the Blair government in the heady early days. The press called the Prime Minister's wife, Cherie Blair, a 'brilliant working mother'. John Pilger remarks: 'This is the same Cherie Booth, barrister, who in 1995 asked a magistrate to return a penniless poll tax defaulter to prison.'[31, 32]

Tony Blair will be remembered above all for the war on Iraq and for drawing Britain into Bush's 'War on Terror'. It is to be hoped that history will judge Blair as harshly as Neville Chamberlain; the weak appeaser of the 1930s who would not risk war in order to stand up to Hitler, and the puppet Prime Minister of the early twenty-first century who sent British troops into combat in a war based on lies out of obedience to an American President. Chamberlain had more to excuse his actions and was the more honourable individual — in as far as politicians are able to be honourable. Blair made Britain as thoroughly an American satellite as any East European state was ever a satellite of the Soviet Union; mass public protests by British citizens failed to change the course the country took just as mass protests by East Germans, Hungarians, Czechs and Poles ultimately failed to change the direction of their countries.

This situation has somewhat improved only because of changes in Washington, just as the East Europeans benefited from changes in Moscow. Bush, America's Brezhnev has — so to speak — been replaced by Obama, America's Gorbachev; the parallel is an inexact one because Obama certainly does not possess Gorbachev's stature and has never brought about changes on the scale of those set in motion by Gorbachev. The Finnish diplomat and scholar Max Jakobson once quoted a remark by President John F. Kennedy: 'The line dividing domestic and foreign affairs has become as indistinct as a line drawn in water.' These words describe Blair's years as Prime Minister, though not exactly in the way in which Kennedy originally used them.

How can we understand the appetite for war of this self-declared Christian Prime Minister, leading a government that still bore the name Labour? We have already noted the zeal with which British leaders starting with Mrs Thatcher have administered capitalism — a sort of bare-knuckle, missionary enthusiasm. Blair was eager to please the arms industry from the day he stepped into 10 Downing Street, especially BAE Systems and its Chairman, Dick Evans, who quickly acquired considerable influence over government actions. The cautious attempts of Robin Cook, the Foreign Secretary, to frame a more ethical foreign policy — including moves to stop the sale of weapons to the murderous regime in Indonesia — were quickly stamped on by Blair in the first year of the new government. Cook was abruptly removed in June 2001 after Blair had won a second General Election.

This was all very consistent with the Thatcher revolution and the way in which British affairs were conducted after the watershed of 1979: Macmillan-Wilson-Heath with the mask dropped and the gloves off. (It is easy to shrug off the politics of 1945 to 1979 as a set of capitalist illusions. However, Orwell was quite aware of the significance of illusions and said so in *The Lion and the Unicorn*: 'An illusion can become a half-truth, a mask can alter the expression of a face... In England such concepts as justice, liberty and objective truth are still believed in. They may be illusions, but they are very powerful illusions. The belief in them influences conduct, national life is different because of them.' And the same was true of the illusions of consensus politics that Mrs Thatcher set out to destroy and succeeded in destroying.)

Nevertheless, Blair sent British forces into action five times in six years; such belligerence was a new departure of his own. About two million British people demonstrated against war in Iraq in February 2003, the largest public protest in British history, coinciding with Blair's fears that Hans Blix and his UN weapons inspectors were winning the argument for indefinite postponement of military action. In a presentation to the UN Security Council on 7 March, intelligent, icy and indignant, Blix described the missiles that the Iraqis were *already destroying*: 'We are not watching the breaking of toothpicks; lethal weapons are being destroyed.' He dismissed the US 'intelligence' on Iraq's chemical and biological weapons capacity as unsupported by any evidence, just as he had already done on 14 February. Blix also pointed out that he and his team needed several more months in Iraq—naturally the Americans and the obedient British ensured that they did not get them.

When Bush ordered the first strikes on 19 March he did not even inform Blair, let alone consult him. Blair's role as America's toady exacted a heavy price in personal credibility and personal dignity. John Kampfner gives an account of Blair's foreign policy from his first days in office to the summer after the invasion of Iraq, which I have found indispensable. Kampfner's book is all the more devastating because he almost entirely refrains from commenting upon the appalling moral implications of the details he reveals. In the first chapter of his book Kampfner comments: '[Blair] was determined to show that he—a Labour Prime Minister—could, and would, do wars. If Winston Churchill and Margaret Thatcher could do them, so could he.'[33]

There is surely a more personal, psychological reason for Blair's craving to be a war leader and a world statesman, necessarily pursued as America's servant—Suez had demonstrated once and for all that Britain could not play international power politics independently of the United States. Rather simple motives and drives almost certainly lay behind what Clare Short called Blair's obsession with his 'place in history'. Jane Fonda points out a simple fact in her autobiography *My Life So Far* (2005), namely that the American Presidents who persisted with the war in Vietnam were men. Fonda asks: 'Why would five administrations, Democratic *and* Republican, knowing... that we couldn't win militarily... choose to postpone failure regardless of how many lives that cost?' Because, she concludes, of the fear of being seen as 'soft', 'a weakling, an appeaser', 'unmanly'. Fonda adds: 'Look at George W. Bush's macho posturing in relation to war.' Look indeed! It is surely relevant to add that Bush and Blair were untalented—to use the kindest possible term—in comparison to the earlier leaders they wished to emulate.

Also, their simplistic religious beliefs must have made their actions easier to carry out. Kampfner records that Blair often had the Bible, the Koran and other religious works beside him as holiday reading. Whatever the nature and quality of Blair's personal beliefs (which do not concern us here), nothing he has said or written as a politician gives the slightest indication that he has any understanding of the religious side of human beings. No doubt Blair would condemn the arch-atheist Karl Marx and Marxism generally, just as Mrs Thatcher did, despite the fact that Marx showed a profound grasp of the essence of religion. The Christianity Blair describes *is* simplistic—God is a sort of large, super-enlightened version of the judges and magistrates to whom Cherie Blair presented her cases in the courts. This is not just Blair's own deficiency, of course; politicians do not possess much spirituality. Some students of religion would say that mainstream, established Christianity has very little spirituality.

The later consequences of the Bush and Blair invasion of Iraq became clear in June 2014. The extreme group ISIS had conquered and occupied large swathes of Iraq, showing themselves to be considerably more ferocious, murderous and ruthless towards many Iraqis than Saddam Hussein had ever been, as well as a potentially far greater danger to the West. Tony Blair's own self-justifying comments on this development were puerile and detached from reality. The one thing that Blair could never admit is how much the original American-British invasion had fuelled support for ISIS. Clare Short, Boris Johnson (the Mayor of London), Blair's former deputy Lord Prescott, Sir Christopher Meyer the British ambassador to America 1997–2003, Lord Ashdown the former Liberal Democrat leader, Michael Stephens of the Royal United Services Institute and the security analyst Eric Grove and others pointed out the direct link between the 2003 invasion and the events of 2014, as well as referring to Blair's lack of grasp on reality. Of course, *some* of Blair's critics had been notably ineffectual in their opposition to the invasion in 2003.

Despite the war in Iraq, and the war in Afghanistan into which Blair led Britain alongside America in October 2001, fifty-two British people died in the bombings in London on 7 July 2005. One of those who carried out the bombings—a man aged thirty from Dewsbury, Yorkshire—recorded a video message before his own death in the attacks, explicitly describing his actions as retaliation for an international war upon the Islamic world by Western governments to which the British people gave their support.[34] And after thirteen years of war, Britain rather ignominiously extricated itself from Afghanistan in 2014, handing over a state of continuing armed conflict to the Afghans.

Apologists for these wars claim that successful terrorist attacks around the world have declined in numbers and have now ceased in Western countries. Of course they have. Anyone who has boarded a plane at an airport since the attacks on the World Trade Centre and the Pentagon of 11 September 2001 knows that security has been massively increased everywhere.

Civil aviation security in America was surprisingly ineffective at the time of the 9/11 attacks (some would say suspiciously ineffective). Increased civil aviation security eventually protected Britain from terrorist attacks by individuals coming from other countries; foreign wars in Islamic countries have only served to recruit terrorists inside Britain.

And so we have reached the aftermath of those wars in Britain today — wars which were justified as a means of making the world safe from terror. A Royal Marine who shot dead a wounded Afghan insurgent in September 2011, saying, 'There you are, shuffle off this mortal coil, you cunt', was found guilty of murder in November 2013. Just three weeks later two men were on trial for the murder of a British soldier in Woolwich on 22 May that year, accused of driving a car into him and then hacking him to death with a cleaver and knives. One of the attackers told police that he was 'a Muslim extremist' fighting against the invasion of Muslim countries and handed over a letter explaining his actions to a witness.[35] Those who are rightly horrified by these events far from always make the connection between them or extend the blame to those leaders who have created the present world situation. The 9/11 attacks and the War on Terror can be seen as a later and worse phase of the Crisis Decades that began in 1973-74 or as a new and more terrible era in modern times. In either case history has led us into a place of darkness.

The murder of the British soldier in Woolwich that was carried out on 22 May 2013, occurring during a time I spent in hospital to which I will return later, and the conviction of a Royal Marine for the murder of a wounded Afghan were by no means the first such events in the spiral of hate and revenge created by Blair and Bush. In September 2005, almost exactly two months after the 7 July bombings, seven British paratroopers were court-martialled, accused of the murder of an Iraqi aged eighteen during the aftermath of the invasion of his country, and were also accused of assaulting two Iraqi women, one of them pregnant and the other who had just given birth, as well as killing a pet dog. When the British Muslim journalist

Yasmin Alibhai-Brown recently wrote the following, the humane intelligence of her newspaper columns over the years and the indignation and revulsion with which she condemned the 7 July bombings added weight to her words:

> Usually, Western soldiers out East break international conventions with impunity... Not all our soldiers are 'heroes'. That's just cant and spin... The truth is that Western armies and governments are not answerable to any overseer. They do what they damn well please. Always have... Civilians have been raped, tortured and murdered by Western allies in Iraq and Afghanistan. We don't even have numbers for them, let alone names.[36, 37]

Naturally, the kind of reaction to the Woolwich murder my fellow patients in hospital displayed and their delight at the marches to be carried out by neo-Nazi groups (more on this later) are far more common than any awareness of the real dynamics of hatred in Britain. Bigotry like theirs provides a reservoir of hysteria to be tapped by future governments in future wars. On the other hand, atrocities by British soldiers recruit more self-styled 'Muslim extremists'. Set against this dismal process are some noble acts of resistance to the tide of outrage and hate, which are often given scant attention or go unreported. The city of Leicester answered the threats of neo-Nazi groups with a demonstration for peace and unity by members of the community of all religions and of no religion.

Meanwhile, disturbing suggestions about the extent to which Blair allowed the Americans to spy on British citizens have surfaced after the revelations by the National Security Agency whistleblower Edward Snowden. No doubt it will be a long time before the full picture emerges—if it ever does—but we can be certain beyond reasonable doubt that yet again those responsible will never suffer for their actions. We can perhaps understand the indignation and bile of the American writer Gore Vidal, a lifelong opponent of American imperial aspirations, in his remark about Britain made to Johann Hari of *The*

Independent, later quoted with relish by Christopher Hitchens: 'This isn't a country, it's an American aircraft carrier.'[38]

It must be said in Blair's favour, however, that he allowed and encouraged the continuation of the peace process in Northern Ireland, which had slowly and painfully begun before he came to office, even if this was done partly to please Bush's predecessor President Clinton, a man who had often vehemently disagreed with John Major over Northern Ireland. Later, the popularity — and the credibility — of Gordon Brown, who succeeded Blair as Prime Minister, seemingly after years of jealous rivalry and hostility, was quickly eroded, partly by the recession that set in after the 2008 global financial and economic crisis (no doubt his time as Chancellor of the Exchequer associated him irrevocably with the banks, which had provoked so much public hostility), and partly by his own incompetence as a political performer. It is a matter of simple decency to refrain from any further comment on Mr Brown.

David Cameron's Conservative-Liberal Coalition took office in 2010 and has declared a fully-fledged economic recovery since the autumn of 2013; this is a predictable claim that is far from entirely convincing. In late January 2014, the Institute for Fiscal Studies contradicted the government's claims, forecasting that average household incomes would be lower in 2015 than in 2010 and lower than before the recession (*The Independent/i*, 25 January 2014). And then, in June 2014, new figures emerged to demonstrate the poverty into which so many British citizens have been driven by successive governments and their running of the economy according to a single ideology of the free market. A study carried out on a scale not previously attempted in the UK, the Poverty and Social Exclusion project, based on interviews with over 14,500 individuals, was undertaken by eight universities and two research agencies. Eighteen million people cannot afford adequate housing; five and a half million adults go without essential clothing; twelve million people cannot afford to take part in many normal social activities; and two and a half million children live in damp homes. Households defined as in a state of poverty have increased from fourteen per cent (about three million) in 1983, when Mrs Thatcher was re-elected, to thirty-three per cent, or 8.7 million, in 2012.

According to this study, and to parallel research by the Joseph Rowntree Foundation, about half the households afflicted by poverty were working families, many of them working forty hours or more each week. Even the new unemployment figures released in July 2014, falling to 2.12 million, were deceptive. John Moylan, the BBC employment and industry correspondent, wrote on 16 July 2014: 'meagre growth in average earnings is in stark contrast to the upbeat news on jobs… [P]ay, which includes bonuses was [at] the lowest growth rate since 2009… pay, which excludes bonuses [was at the] lowest growth rate since records began in 2001.'

The British government continues to preside over a country in which several thousand people in a year go to hospital because of malnutrition; almost a million people are fed by food banks in the face of protests by six hundred church leaders (*The Independent*, 16 April 2014); with Lord Adebowale lamenting the detention of 54,000 people under mental health laws and the use of police cells for the mentally ill; Atos Healthcare had bullied the sick and disabled to go to work on the basis of flawed assessments; the 'bedroom tax' is pushing people into greater and greater hardship, while bailiffs exceed their legal powers when trying to extract money from people who cannot pay their debts. There is more to Britain than this, of course. And yet these things are the experiences that combine to deform and damage the lives of many of us. Would the young people who survived the deluge of death that was the Second World War have believed what lay in store in late middle age for the babies they conceived and brought into the world in the first years of peace? Would they have believed just what kind of road their country was to travel in the next seventy years?

[1] Eric Hobsbawm, *Age of Extremes: The Short Twentieth Century 1914–1991*, London, 1994; *Interesting Times: A Twentieth Century Life*, London, 2002.

[2] Geoffrey Roberts, *Stalin's Wars: From World War to Cold War, 1939–1953*, New Haven & London, 2006.
[3] Eric Hobsbawm, *Age of Extremes: The Short Twentieth Century 1914–1991*, London, 1994.
[4] Max Jakobson, *Finland in the New Europe*, New Haven, 1998. Jakobson, a Finnish scholar, is a long-serving diplomat.
[5] David Runciman, *The Politics of Good Intentions*, Princeton & Oxford, 2006.
[6] Philip A. Thomas, 'Legislative Responses to Terrorism' in *Beyond September 11: An Anthology of Dissent*, edited by Phil Scraton, London, 2002.
[7] S. Marglin and J. Schor, editors, *The Golden Age of Capitalism*, Oxford, 1990.
[8] Krishan Kumar, 'The Social and Cultural Setting', in *The New Pelican Guide to English Literature, Volume 8: The Present*, edited by Boris Ford, Harmondsworth, 1983.
[9] Gerry Conlon, *Proved Innocent*, London, 1990.
[10] Mark Curtis, *The Ambiguities of Power: British Foreign Policy since 1945*, London, 1995; *Web of Deceit; Britain's Real Role in the World*, London, 2003.
[11] John Pilger, *Freedom Next Time*, London, 2006.
[12] *Revealing the Mind Bender General* by James Maw, BBC Radio 4, broadcast 1 April 2009 and 17 March 2010 (http://www.jamesmaw.co.uk, last accessed on 17 March 2011).
[13] Anthony James, *Amputated Souls: The Psychiatric Assault on Liberty 1935–2011*, Exeter, 2013.
[14] Alan Palmer, *The Penguin Dictionary of Twentieth Century History*, Harmondsworth, 1979.
[15] Amnesty International, *Report on Torture*, New York, 1975.
[16] Peter Wright, *Spycatcher*, New York, 1987.
[17] Martin Jacques and Francis Mulhern (editors) *The Forward March of Labour Halted?*, London, 1981; Eric Hobsbawm, *Politics for a Rational Left*, London, 1989.
[18] Eric Hobsbawm, *Interesting Times: A Twentieth Century Life*, London, 2002.
[19] Margaret Thatcher, *The Downing Street Years*, London, 1993.
[20] United Nations Development Programme, *Human Development Report*, New York, 1997.
[21] United Nations Development Programme, *Human Development Report*, Oxford, 1992.
[22] Carey Oppenheim and Lisa Harker, *Poverty, the Facts*, Child Poverty Action Group, 1996.
[23] 'Children in Statistics', *Index on Censorship*, February 1997.
[24] Government Statistical Service, *DSS Households Below Average Income: A Statistical Analysis, 1979–1992/3*, HMSO, 1995.

[25] *Economic Trends, December 94*, HMSO, 1994.
[26] Pamela Abbott and Claire Wallace, *The Family and the New Right*, London, 1992.
[27] Stephen Blake and Andrew John, *Iron Lady: The Thatcher Years*, London, 2003, 2012, 2013.
[28] Seumas Milne, *The Enemy Within: MI5, Maxwell and the Scargill Affair*, London, 1994, 1995, 2004.
[29] Johann Hari, 'Unrepentant Irishman', *The Independent*, Wednesday 9 September 2009.
[30] Peter Mandelson and Roger Liddle, *The Blair Revolution: Can New Labour Deliver?*, London, 1996.
[31] John Pilger, *Hidden Agendas*, London, 1998.
[32] Hugh MacPherson in *Tribune,* 30 May 1997.
[33] John Kampfner, *Blair's Wars*, London, 2003.
[34] Kim Sengupta, *The Independent*, 3 September 2005.
[35] Paul Peachey, *The Independent/i*, 30 November 2013.
[36] Kim Sengupta, *The Independent*, 6 September 2005.
[37] Yasmin Alibhai-Brown, 'Western brutality in all its horror: the shocking murder committed by Marine A speaks of wider attitudes', *The Independent/i*, 11 November 2013.
[38] Christopher Hitchens, *Arguably*, London, 2011.

Chapter Two

The Dragon in the Garage

We have recently seen Scotland vote against independence from the UK. However, a large number of Scots will remain disenchanted with the idea of being British. And the consequences of that disenchantment cannot be foreseen. We should now devote some space to considering that other non-English part of the UK—Wales. I believe that this examination will tell us something about Britain and its possible future.

The British general election campaign of 2010 will be remembered (if at all) for its cautiously buoyant sense that anything—or at least, a great deal more than usual—was possible. However, it would be more correct to say that this mood was strong in England and Scotland, while in Wales it became apparent that it was not likely that there would be very much that was new or different on the horizon. ITV 1 Wales screened Welsh versions of the political leaders' debate, although they were only very pale imitations of the Brown-Cameron-Clegg event. During the second debate, Peter Hain, then New Labour's Secretary of State for Wales—once a radical left-winger, but transformed into the most dutiful Blairite—justified the war in Afghanistan in words that might have been taken directly from the speeches of ex-President George W. Bush. This issue had already been called 'a big, blood-spattered hole we are all supposed to ignore' by the *Independent* journalist Johann Hari.[1] The other participants in the debate listened in bland silence and expressed no dissent, fitting themselves to a posture that has become entirely predictable, and which rather confirmed how right Hari had been. Clearly, English silence also extended into Wales. There was also complete silence on an issue that was more specific to Wales, namely, the possibility that the country might seek a separate destiny as a fully independent member state of the European Union. The issue was mentioned by no one, not even to dismiss or condemn it, and this must have made an odd impression on many of us who recall the 1970s and 1980s, when full independence was frequently declared to be the goal of the Welsh Nationalists. Two of Hain's fellow participants, Cheryl Gillan, the Conservative Shadow Welsh Secretary, and the Welsh Liberal Democrat leader, Kirsty Williams, could hardly be expected to refer to the issue, but the third participant was the Plaid Cymru (Welsh Nationalist) leader Ieuan Wyn Jones. The existence of a devolved Welsh Assembly has obviously not promoted ideas of independence—quite the opposite.

The question of Welsh independence has been removed from mainstream political discourse and debate, although the nationalists presumably find this an unpalatable fact to face. This fact is amply demonstrated, however, by examining the Plaid Cymru 2010 Westminster Manifesto entitled *Think Different. Think Plaid* alongside *Elect a local champion*, the 2010 Manifesto of the Scottish National Party—the differences are glaring! (These documents were available in paper/printed form and could be downloaded from the internet throughout the election campaign.) The Plaid Cymru Manifesto states: 'Plaid calls on any incoming Westminster government to agree a request for a referendum on law making powers by the National Assembly... Plaid Cymru also believes that, in time, further powers may be transferred to the National Assembly beginning with the police and criminal justice, and followed by energy and broadcasting' (p. 4). There is a return to this theme on page 17: 'We want our National Assembly to have the tools it needs to do the job—to make a real difference to people's lives. To do this Wales needs proper powers.' There is only one reference to independence, being the only use of the word 'independence/independent' in the entire document, occurring on page 32: 'Plaid Cymru is committed to an independent Wales as a full member of the European Union.' However, this document of thirty-five pages makes no mention of any strategy for attaining independence, calling only for increased powers for a devolved assembly within the United Kingdom.

The 2010 Manifesto of the Scottish National Party makes for very different reading. The word 'independence/independent' occurs three times on page 5 in the introduction by the SNP leader Alex Salmond. Pages 17 to 23 of the SNP Manifesto are devoted to independence, including the words, 'Together we see ourselves as a nation and independence is the natural state for nations like ours... Independence runs like a golden thread through this manifesto...' on page 22.

Why, then, after the same period during which both Wales and Scotland had devolved assemblies, was full independence regarded so differently by the nationalist parties of these two nations? The political, indeed the *electoral*, reasons for this difference are obvious at a glance. The political parties held the following number of seats in the National Assembly in Wales in April 2010: Labour 26, Plaid Cymru 14, Welsh Conservatives 13, Welsh Liberal Democrats 6, with one independent member. The Welsh Assembly Government was a coalition of Labour and Plaid Cymru, with Plaid's Ieuan Wyn Jones as Deputy First Minister, and although the two coalition parties held a press conference on 20 April 2010 in which they did not even mention the UK General Election, a brutally candid statement by Professor Mark Drakeford (who would be a candidate for the Welsh Assembly) had already appeared, suggesting that Labour would do well to keep open the possibility of a coalition with the Liberal Democrats after the Assembly elections in 2011.[2]

In Scotland, the minority SNP government headed by Alex Salmond had no such worries, which presumably gave the SNP Manifesto its confident and ambitious tone. In comparison to the Welsh predicament, the situation in the Scottish Assembly stood out in sharp contrast, with the parties enjoying the following representation: Scottish National Party 47, Scottish Labour 46, Scottish Conservative and Unionist Party 16, Scottish Liberal Democrats 16, Scottish Green Party 2, with one independent member and one member of no party affiliation. Nevertheless, a political and electoral explanation for the differing strength of aspirations to independence in Scotland and Wales only pushes the question a step away without answering it. Why do the Welsh vote so differently from the Scots?

Ultimately, the answer to the above question must lie in the sphere of national and cultural identity, intimately involving these nations' respective perceptions of themselves, and in exploring such matters—in the case of Wales—it will be necessary to leave the relatively sure ground of electoral politics, or even economics, and move into the far more subjective and speculative area of cultural studies. This is the territory we shall need to traverse, however, in order to arrive at a tentative understanding of the dynamics of potential or actual change in Wales. But firstly, two other political facts (also unpalatable to many politicians in Wales today) need to be considered.

Firstly, Wales has never prospered by being part of the United Kingdom, and more disturbingly, there is very considerable evidence that the existence of the devolved Welsh Assembly has done little or nothing to improve matters fundamentally. The severe unemployment of the 1930s and the 1980s struck some areas of Britain cruelly and affected other areas very little, and Wales was one of the worst afflicted areas. Further, when the coalmining industry was largely dismantled in the 1980s as a matter of calculated government policy, Wales was once again particularly badly affected. The disadvantaged status of the Welsh became so widely known that a travel guide on Western Europe, part of a very non-political series of travel books originating in Australia, stated in 1999:

> Wales has had the misfortune to be so close to England that it could not be allowed its independence, and yet far enough away to be conveniently forgotten. It sometimes feels like England's unloved back yard—a suitable place for mines, pine plantations and nuclear power stations. Even the most enduring

> of its symbols—the grim mining towns and powerful castles—represent exploitation and colonialism... Huge swathes of the countryside have been vandalised by mining, grossly insensitive forestry operations and power lines...[3]

This is a description, produced partly by authors born outside the UK and therefore all the more objective, that is all too familiar to those of us who live in Wales or know it well, although, for political reasons, its accuracy would not always be acknowledged too loudly.

A far more intimate and damning survey was produced by Gareth H. Williams, Professor of Sociology at the University of Salford, and also published in 1999, at a time of high hopes attending the prospect of the Welsh Assembly becoming a reality. Professor Williams pointed out that:

> Disease and premature death have been woven into the fabric of Welsh society during the twentieth century... In mining communities the routine burden of illness and death... was punctuated, as at Senghenydd in 1913 and Aberfan in 1966, by catastrophic loss of life... [H]ealth in Wales remains poor compared with most European neighbours... The death rate in Wales has increased relative to that in England over the last decade, and although the infant mortality rate has fallen by over a half in the last twenty years, it remains higher than most of the rest of Europe... [M]ajor determinants of ill-health [are] occupation and employment, the levels and distribution of income, education and housing conditions... [W]ithin Wales... areas with high levels of morbidity and mortality from cancer and coronary heart disease are [those] where unemployment rates are rising, where house prices are falling most dramatically, where a high proportion of the housing is unfit, and where more than a third of school children in primary school are entitled to free school meals.[4]

With Professor Williams we seem to be back in the late Victorian era! His article is powerful, however, in courageously stating connections between social conditions and health that are obvious, and also in applying generally accepted connections *to Wales specifically*—an application that was far from generally accepted in 1999, and is still not fully accepted now. One of the chief sources used by Professor Williams, who was the Deputy Director of the Public Health Research and Resource Centre at the University of Salford, might have come as a surprise to some politicians in Wales—it was the independent report by Sir Donald Acheson and his group published in London in 1998, which stressed that poor health in Wales was related to 'the fact that the country has the lowest level of personal income in the UK—by a wide margin that is getting wider'.[5] The last sixteen years have overlaid a concluding remark by Professor Williams with a certain irony: 'At this point in Welsh history the key opportunity structure is the National Assembly.'

If—to use a piece of current jargon—we 'scroll forward' eleven years to the 2010 General Election (and some sixteen years to the present), we find some rather depressing, but convincing, evidence of just what the devolved assembly made of its opportunities. On 19 April 2010, the UK Competitiveness Index (UKCI) released its current study of the twelve regions and nations of the UK about which it had been amassing data since 1997. Wales was conclusively found to be the least competitive of these areas by the UKCI, which relied on an array of facts including spending on research and development, business start-up rates, exports per head of the population, hourly productivity, gross weekly pay and unemployment rates. Some of the conclusions of Professor Robert Huggins, who wrote the report with Dr Piers Thompson, were bleak indeed:

> This highlights the increasingly desperate state our economy [in Wales] has fallen into… Wales is becoming increasingly detached… There is little evidence that devolution and the establishment of the Welsh Assembly is contributing to improved competitiveness. In fact, the opposite appears to be largely true… Wales should look to nations such as Finland, where its economic development strategy is signed up to by all parties, and remains in place regardless of changes in power.

> This more mature and patient approach has helped Finland become one of the world's most competitive nations... In Switzerland, for instance, politicians tend to be individuals who have already achieved significant international and national influence in other careers, and enter politics later as a form of civic responsibility. Perhaps this is a model the Assembly should be encouraged to emulate.[6]

Interestingly, the Scottish National Party looked with approval to the model of Norway, the near neighbour of both Finland and of Scotland itself, in the matter of energy products to generate national wealth and in military matters (the Norwegians have always kept all nuclear weapons off their soil), when they wrote their 2010 Manifesto (pp. 11 and 21).

Returning to the UKCI report, we see that the authors found that the least competitive localities in Britain were all in Wales. It is fair to assume that all mainstream politicians in Wales felt that it was as wise to avoid mentioning the report as it would have been to avoid touching a live hand grenade. (Those readers who have stayed with me to this point will have noticed that the effort to see Britain in the context of Europe and against the background of the mosaic of European culture is a connecting thread in this book. Orwell also wrote of British culture as part of the Western tradition. We live at a time when traditional British suspicion and contempt for Europe may once again determine our future. When we look at the countries just mentioned, it is useful to remember that strong cultural links exist between Norway and Scotland and northern England—quite apart from globalization, the European Economic Area and the European Union—and Norway has a common border with both Finland and Sweden. Methods used by Britain's neighbours could be used by the British. Furthermore, those with a Marxist outlook do not always pay enough attention to the fact that capitalist political systems vary enormously—some of them are a great deal worse than others!)

A second political fact is uncomfortable for many people in Wales, both for politicians and for those outside politics, namely, that there is no rational or practical obstacle to the existence of an entirely independent Wales *as a member state of the European Union*. I have emphasized European membership because the recent history of Ireland provides such a close and suggestive parallel. Ireland became independent in 1922, but as the Irish Free State it was intensely conservative, socially and economically, and above all on sexual and religious issues, and these tendencies derived not just from the establishment of the Free State, but also from the assassination of Michael Collins (a consequence of that settlement), the leader who had embodied a more secular, humanist and modern strand in Irish national life, followed by the ascendancy of the authoritarian and conservative Eamon de Valera. Above all, Ireland was typically post-colonial in its economic backwardness and extensive dependence on trade with Britain. When the Republic became a member of the European Union (then the EEC) in 1973, 'the engine that has driven all other components of change', as Brian Arkins called it,[7] the way was irreversibly open to the spectacular prosperity of the 1990s.

That prosperity coincided with the incumbency of President Mary Robinson, who reflected a new image of themselves back to the Irish, making possible the development of a more liberal, progressive Ireland, a kind of sixth Scandinavian country. (Recalling the Swiss model referred to above, Robinson had certainly achieved influence—as a human rights lawyer and constitutional expert—before standing for election.) Putting prejudices aside, it is very difficult to conceive of any valid reason why Wales should not follow a similar path within Europe, except, of course, for one: that very same issue of national self-image, self-esteem and identity, which will lead us into the much more subjective realm of Welsh culture and self-expression.

At a literary event in Cardiff in 1986, a respected Marxist historian made the following remark to me, speaking of a very radical journal published in Welsh: 'Of course, nobody actually reads it! The working class, even the militant trade unionists, don't read it because it's in Welsh. And the Welsh-speaking Welsh don't read it because it's left-wing and Marxist.' This comment was not entirely attributable to the historian's notoriously dry sense of humour, and if it was an exaggeration it was not a very great one. There is no doubt that we could partly trace the shape of Welsh culture and society back to the medieval world, but the developments of the last two hundred years are the most relevant and must concern us most.

Since industrialization, the force for political change in Wales has come mainly through the trade unions, the Labour Party and a left-wing outlook. (Engels found it significant to quote a speech by W. Bevan, President of the TUC, at a meeting in Swansea in 1887, when writing the preface to the 1888 English edition of *The Communist Manifesto*.) A huge psychological vacuum has been created by the retreat of heavy industry, the discrediting of party politics generally and the decline of any deep loyalty to the Labour Party.

The longing for some form of national independence has been *largely*—it is a matter of emphasis, but a very strong emphasis—a rural phenomenon among Welsh speakers or among academics, intellectuals and writers who usually (but not always) express themselves in Welsh. The most typically Welsh political leader to become famous in Britain as a whole was the left-wing Labour MP Aneurin Bevan (1897–1960), but when he spoke of the alien atmosphere in the House of Commons in which 'his people… were shut out from all this; were forbidden to take part in the dramatic scenes depicted in these frescoes', he was *not* referring to the Welsh, but instead to the working class.[8] And Bevan's famously passionate vitriol, 'No attempt… can eradicate from my heart a deep burning hatred… So far as I am concerned they are lower than vermin', was directed at the Tory Party, not at the English.[9]

By contrast, the poet Saunders Lewis (1893–1984) wrote in Welsh, converted to Roman Catholicism, longed for the hierarchic and traditionalist values of the Middle Ages, was one of the founders of Plaid Cymru, and committed a symbolic act of arson (for which he was imprisoned in Wormwood Scrubs) in order to protest against the presence of an RAF base in Wales. Lewis was also the president of Plaid Cymru from 1926 to 1939, standing as a (defeated) parliamentary candidate for the party in 1943.[10]

Those who represent the mainstream political parties in Wales today are not, of course, as dramatically different as Bevan and Lewis were, but the traditions were established early on and still retain some of their character and complexion. Widely supported, reforming, urban socialism and predominantly rural, Welsh-speaking nationalism have proved very difficult to draw together into a political movement with a common agenda and shared objectives.

Returning to culture, we find that the only Welsh writer with a truly international reputation, Dylan Thomas (1914–1953), wrote in English, was born in suburban Swansea, lived in London for long periods and was quite indifferent to Welsh nationalism and to politics in general. The most famous Welsh poet of recent decades is R.S. Thomas (1913–2000) — he was not related to Dylan Thomas — an Anglican cleric whose aggressive Welsh nationalism attracted attention, whereas his poetry — written in English — was not primarily concerned with nationalism. Unlike R.S. Thomas, who lived in rural Wales, and whose poems reflect philosophical and existential concerns more than political ones, John Tripp, coming to prominence in Wales in the 1960s, dealt with 'unemployment, derelict industrial sites, TV, booze, ignorant hedonism and a merciless Nature', while longing for an 'almost inconceivable un-anglicized, de-industrialized Wales, for a country brought up on Dafydd ap Gwilym, Lowell, Saunders Lewis, *Planet* and Solzhenitsyn, and not *The Sun* and *Emmerdale Farm*'.[11] These longings, vaguely reminiscent of those of D.H. Lawrence or of Solzhenitsyn himself for their own societies, are somewhat self-indulgent and unrealistic in any culture. It is painful to point out that they are especially remote from the reality of life in Wales.

So much, we might say, for Wales expressing itself through literature or high culture, but what about work that enters the popular mainstream, such as the cinema, for instance? It is instructive here to consider two films, one Scottish and one Welsh, released within roughly a year of each other, just as devolution was about to come to both nations, and both of them enjoying some considerable box office success and publicity.

The Scottish film is *Trainspotting* (1996), directed by Danny Boyle, and the Welsh film is *Twin Town* (1997), directed by Kevin Allen, and both films reject national stereotypes and deal with national self-image. *Trainspotting* is considered to be a nihilistic film, and Renton, one of the main characters, utters the now famous words 'there are no reasons', but he also comments with angry eloquence on Scotland's relationship with England. The film came at a pivotal moment in Scotland's history, establishing artistic independence from the British cinema and a new kind of national self-image; as Emma Anne James observes in a recent study: 'That is what makes *Trainspotting* so unique in national cinema studies, it came before the political changes, art influenced life, not the other way round... [T]he one factor the group [Renton and his friends] has in common is being Scottish... [T]hey have no real unifying factor outside their nationality.'[12]

Whether or not *Twin Town* succeeds as a comedy, whether or not it is funny, is something that must be left to individual taste, but more importantly, it must be said that if *Trainspotting* is 'nihilistic', then *Twin Town* is infinitely more nihilistic. It is set in Swansea and tells a story in which every one of the characters is either very stupid or completely corrupt, and sometimes both, seeming to be an exercise in depicting — but not satirizing, because it has no detached or outside view — England's most derisive view of the Welsh and the most self-mutilating Welsh vision of Wales: dishonesty, corruption, stupidity and immature weakness. The characters have none of the intelligence, anger or vitality of Renton and his friends in *Trainspotting*, and there is no equivalent to Renton's angry tirade about the relationship with England. The only reference to Welsh national identity is made by a character who is outwitting a corrupt police officer, and this is expressed in terms of rivalry with England on the rugby field. Considering the popularity of the film in Wales, it must be seen as reflecting an aspect of the Welsh self-image just as much as the recent manifesto of Plaid Cymru.

It is not so very far to move from the products of culture to the most fundamental element that underlies culture, language itself. This, I suggest, is a uniquely painful subject in Wales, when it is discussed objectively, because of the enormous iconic and sentimental status given to the Welsh language. There are, very roughly, 500,000 people who speak Welsh, but I further suggest that no precise figure is available, because the ability to speak or use Welsh cannot be clearly defined, particularly in the south of the country. There are, of course, people who can speak Welsh fluently and correctly and take pride in doing so. It is extremely common, however, for people who think of themselves as able to speak Welsh to be quite unable to utter a complex sentence without interjecting English words; while the use of signs in public places in Welsh brings home the shockingly corrupt state of the language. In libraries, the shelf on which Westerns are kept will be labelled *cowbois*, despite the fact that the Welsh word for 'cow' is *buwch*. 'Golf course' is *cwrs golff* and 'lift', as in between floors, is *lifft*; while even educated Welsh people will sometimes declare that Welsh is 'the purest language in Europe' or 'the oldest language in Europe', which is demonstrably absurd from the point of view of history and comparative linguistics.

It is interesting to compare this approach to language to that of Iceland. In Icelandic, 'computer' is *tolva* (number prophetess), 'telephone' is *simi* (the long thread) and 'radio' is *utvarp*. Far from reinforcing a distinct sense of identity, Welsh all too often functions as something that further dilutes that identity. It is not a question of there being a majority of Scots or Irish citizens fluently speaking the much purer Scottish Gaelic language or Irish Gaelic language, strengthening national identity or adherence to political independence—obviously there is no such linguistic majority in these countries. The problem for identity, self-image and self-esteem in Wales is that 'Welsh', for all practical purposes, is quite often a dialect of English with some Welsh words thrown in, creating a situation in which many people who confidently believe that they 'speak Welsh' cannot even find the original words for numbers greater than ten and resort to English instead, possessing, in fact, a not much greater grasp of Welsh than some enterprising British holiday-makers have of Spanish or French.

George Orwell, with characteristic bluntness, said in *The English People*: 'In any circumstances that we can foresee, the proletariat of Hammersmith will not arise and massacre the bourgeoisie of Kensington: they are not different enough.' We might adapt Orwell's insight to the situation in Wales as follows. In any circumstances that we can foresee, the Welsh people are unlikely to develop enough enthusiasm for independence from England to make it a reality: they are not different enough.

I took the title of this chapter from a thought exercise used by the American scientist Carl Sagan (1934–1996) in his book *The Demon-Haunted World* (1996). How would we react, Sagan asked, to someone's claim that a dragon lived in his/her garage? Perhaps we would ask to see the dragon, only to be told that it is invisible, that it floats in the air without leaving foot-prints, that it is heatless and cannot be detected by infrared sensors, and finally that it is incorporeal. We would begin to ask what difference there is between having a dragon of this kind in the garage and having no dragon at all. This chapter is devoted to the proposition that in the absence of a nationalist party with any credible strategy to create a sovereign state, and in the absence of popular enthusiasm for sovereignty or even a deeply held sense of separate identity, the Welsh dragon will remain securely locked in the garage.

A 'new form of government' was allegedly installed in Westminster by the 2010 General Election. One of the few reassuring aspects of that rather strange and unstable election was the fact that the parties of the extreme right (together with their unwitting or covert allies in the anti-European lobby) made little or no headway. The Conservatives enjoyed a modest revival in Wales, having been erased from the electoral map in recent elections; clearly Welsh voters moved somewhat away from Labour and the Liberal Democrats and somewhat nearer to the Conservatives. There remained the brutal fact that Wales elected only three Plaid Cymru MPs to Westminster. The wind of change may have seemed to blow through the 2010 General Election, but it did not blow in the direction of Welsh nationalism or breathe any new life into the Welsh dragon.

[1] Johann Hari, 'The shameful, bloody silence at the heart of the election', *The Independent*, 16 April 2010.
[2] *Western Mail*, 17 April 2010, quoting *Agenda*, journal of the Institute of Welsh Affairs.
[3] *Lonely Planet Western Europe*, Victoria, Australia, fourth edition, 1999.
[4] Gareth H. Williams, *Iechyd Da?* [Good Health?], *Planet: The Welsh Internationalist*, Issue 133, February/March 1999.
[5] *Independent Inquiry into Inequalities in Health Report*, Chairman: Sir Donald Acheson, London, HMSO, 1998.
[6] Robert Huggins and Piers Thompson, *UK Competitiveness Index 2010*, Centre for International Competitiveness, University of Wales Institute, Cardiff, 2010; also, *Western Mail*, 19 April 2010.
[7] Brian Arkins, 'Tiger-Talk, the transformation of Ireland', *Planet: The Welsh Internationalist*, Issue 133, February/March 1999.
[8] Aneurin Bevan, *In Place of Fear*, London, 1952.
[9] Aneurin Bevan, Speech at Manchester, 4 July 1949.
[10] Joseph P. Clancy's 'Introduction and Notes' to his translation of the *Selected Poems* of Saunders Lewis gives a particularly sensitive account of the poet's turbulent career.
[11] Robert Minhinnick, 'Our Last Romantic: A Reading of John Tripp', *Poetry Wales*, Volume 22, Number 1, 1986.
[12] Emma Anne James, *Reversing the 'British Gaze'*, Hugh Owen Library, University of Aberystwyth, 2010.

Chapter Three

The Monarchy, 'Stick with Nurse...'

Not so very long before starting work on this book, I had a heated conversation with a woman of about my age, an educated lady with a lively intellect who had once run her own translation agency and had later become a qualified archaeologist. She mentioned a certain wedding and the possibility of public street parties to celebrate it. I said something rather scathing and uncharitable about the street parties. The lady demanded to know:

> 'If people want to hold street parties, why do you want to prevent them?'

Immediately, I sensed that a whiff of anathematization was in the air and that I was in danger of tainting myself with the heresies of Tony Benn and Arthur Scargill (excellent company), Ralph Miliband (who allegedly left 'an evil legacy') and, recently—since the publication of her novel for adults *The Casual Vacancy*—J.K. Rowling (wonderful company—I only wished I deserved the association). Tolstoy was anathematized by the Russian Orthodox Church, in Britain individuals such as those just mentioned are anathematized by the holy offices of the *Daily Mail*. I hastened to make my position clear. In my opinion—I said—if these two young people wanted to demonstrate their commitment to each other by getting married, then that was a matter that should be of no interest to any sensible person other than their families and friends, after all, neither of them had yet achieved anything of any particular distinction.

The lady told me that the young husband-to-be was very good at the job he was currently doing. I could not help pointing out that a local postmistress I knew had a daughter who had served in Afghanistan as an RAF nurse; this young woman would probably get married within the next year or two, but no one would hold street parties to mark the occasion. As for preventing people holding street parties, I had no wish to do so, and I would not do so even if I had the power. However, as a fellow citizen, I was entitled to express my dismay that people might spend their time on such activities, just as I am dismayed that people spend their time reading *The Sun* and watching television soap operas. I am all for frequent parties; having lived in Spain, I had watched entire communities launch themselves into four-day fiestas at least three times a year, without — necessarily — celebrating anyone's wedding and certainly not in adulation of well-known people.

My libertarian values seemed to reassure the lady, and the evening continued amicably. And yet there, in our conversation, lay one of the most important aspects of the subject of the monarchy. In Britain there lives a large family: a grandmother, a grandfather, sons and a daughter who once had 'fairytale' marriages that have not been outstandingly successful or happy, grandsons grown to adulthood. The family has enjoyed boundless wealth, privilege and educational opportunities. One daughter-in-law developed from a rather silly young woman into a serious and humane campaigner, offending the conventions of the family, frightening the elected and unelected British political elite and the international arms industry. She died in circumstances that some responsible and intelligent commentators and a great number of 'ordinary people' still find suspicious. Apart from this young woman, the family is not particularly interesting and shows less ability than the majority of large families. If they were a family of wealthy bankers or business people they would attract no notice at all, except perhaps as the objects of society gossip.

A great many of the arguments used to justify the monarchy are very similar in substance to an assertion I once heard my mother make. When I was a little boy I once asked my (then) very right-wing mother why we should stand when 'God Save the Queen' was played in the cinema. My mother said grandly and witheringly: 'Because the Queen is your sovereign lady.' There are a great many circular arguments of this kind; if you ask some people *why* they think Africans are inferior, they will say: 'Because they are just Africans.' And if you ask some believers how we *know* that the Bible is the revealed word of God, they will tell you: 'Because it says so in the Bible.' When you strip away grand phrases, many arguments in favour of the monarchy turn out to be circular in much the same way.

Interestingly enough, my mother—who was an intelligent woman, although not a very pleasant person—evolved into what would be called an angry left-winger in middle and old age; she also became a vitriolic anti-monarchist and ardent republican, and she had nothing to gain from this change—she had no career and no influence beyond her immediate family. She seemed deeply disappointed and infuriated by the political system she had once believed in. Even more interesting, perhaps, is the fact that the change began when Margaret Thatcher was elected to power in 1979. My mother idolized Churchill, had listened to Churchill's speeches on the 'wireless' and survived the intensive Nazi bombing of Swansea, but the ideology of Mrs Thatcher seems to have been more than she could stomach. It often happens that a loss of faith in one manifestation of a political system brings disillusionment with the whole edifice.

Prince Charles, who is now, after the Queen, the most prominent member of the Royal Family, moved my mother to anger in particular. I also remember a Latin teacher from my childhood, a genuine right-wing ex-army officer and an official of the local Conservative Party. This teacher used to tell a funny story in one line: 'There was once a cavalry officer who was so stupid that even his fellow cavalry officers noticed.' I sometimes recall this story when I hear of Prince Charles, substituting 'member of the Royal Family' for 'cavalry officer' and 'other members of his family' for 'fellow officers'. However, this is unjust. The Prince does not entirely deserve the scathing contempt of the frequently superb essayist Christopher Hitchens either (comparable in venom to comments by my mother).

Some of the pronouncements Charles has indulged in over the years have been blazingly silly, but his remarks on climate change deniers in a speech at an awards ceremony at Buckingham Palace at the end of January 2014 were admirably sensible. Here he supported the findings of science. Hitchens rightly attacked the Prince's very, very silly remarks on Galileo in 2010. It might be a good idea if the heir to the throne read one of the excellent books by the Cambridge physicist and science editor Joanne Baker, one of the many fine popularizers of science that Britain has produced—perhaps he has subsequently done so.

As far back as 1982, Prince Charles stated: 'The whole imposing edifice of modern medicine… is like the celebrated Tower of Pisa: slightly off-balance.' This is largely true, especially if we include psychiatry, which is ignorant and callous pseudo-medicine. If Charles showed a naïve enthusiasm for homeopathy, then it must also be said that the drug companies exercise great influence over the actions and thinking of doctors. As the health service in Britain is denied the resources to provide widely accessible care on the level of the Soviet Union in the 1950s or tiny, besieged, revolutionary Cuba in the 1980s, the quick results offered by mainstream therapies are perpetually in favour. (Anyone who doubts this comparison should read a biography of Solzhenitsyn, who suffered from and was successfully cured of severe cancer in the 1950s, while he was a former political prisoner still under surveillance, or the essay on Cuba written by Germaine Greer for *Women: A World Report* published by the UN.)

And here is Prince Charles writing a Foreword to a collection of essays celebrating the 350th anniversary of The Book of Common Prayer in 2012: 'Who was it who decided that for people who aren't very good at reading, the best things to read are those written by people who aren't very good at writing... banality is for nobody. It might be accessible for all, but so is a desert.' This is well said and very true—it would presumably have been ignored by Hitchens who detested both the monarchy and religion, and bravely faced his own death in a spirit of unshakeable atheism the year before the Prince's words were published. (Hitchens was the arch-enemy of the British Royal Family and his arguments are frequently conclusive when considered honestly; sadly, he dwells spitefully on the Prince's physical appearance, which is great fun—unless you happen to be Charles and his family—but quite unworthy as political commentary.)

Nevertheless, even the best of the Prince's criticisms are not above the level we would expect from a middling, reasonably clever newspaper columnist. This is the pinnacle of the intellectual achievement of the Royal Family as far as we can ascertain: we can only go on what is known publicly. The endlessly repeated claims that the Queen has 'great knowledge' and an 'astute understanding' of world affairs are based on necessarily private and undisclosed conversations. These claims are almost always made by politicians with a personal interest in voicing such judgements, and they are echoed by writers who support the monarchy. Also, the political leaders who have met the Queen and praise her in this way are usually unimpressive in their own mental processes as well as seriously deficient in the basic honesty of the average person.

It is worth adding that Prince Charles put on wellington boots and visited Somerset in February 2014, seeing for himself the areas devastated by the winter floods and criticizing the fact that it had taken so long for the government to provide effective help, a little reminiscent of the condemnation of poverty and unemployment in South Wales by Edward VIII. This can be dismissed as a public relations exercise by a man who would be King in the near future. However, at least the heir to the throne bothered to go. Cameron, a Prime Minister uncomfortably upstaged by Charles—and a man rapidly leaving behind his slender humane credentials in a pursuit of re-election squalid even by current political standards—lamely copied the visit three days later, right down to the wellington boots.

Contemporary Review was founded in 1866 and reached its third century of continuous publication. The journal specialized in international affairs, politics, the environment and current literary issues and was read in over sixty countries. I had the pleasure of seeing several of my essays published in the *Review* over the years, and I naturally read other contributions with the keenest interest. The June 2012 issue of *Contemporary Review* (Volume 294, number 1705) contained an article entitled 'The Queen's Diamond Jubilee' by James Munson, the historical biographer and literary editor of *CR*. It is a tribute to the integrity of the journal that Munson's article was published alongside an icily factual and restrained piece on the Palestinian struggle for survival by Hafizullah Emadi; a thoughtful, brilliantly written reappraisal of Harold Wilson by Geoffrey Heptonstall; a wonderfully challenging reflection on *All Quiet on the Western Front* and the introduction of children to violence in literature by Chris Arthur; and an essay of my own on Solzhenitsyn. Munson squarely supports the monarchy and his article is a defence of that institution and a tribute to the present Queen and her family. His essay, self-consciously learned and impatient of intellectual imprecision and muddle, can therefore be seen as a good example of serious monarchist thinking that is worth citing in any discussion of the monarchy. James Munson also defends and supports the Church of England and its ties with the monarchy.

Some books are reviewed in the course of Mr Munson's essay, all of them written by individuals of royalist persuasion. Sarah Bradford calls the Queen a 'living representative of sixty years of our history'. Perhaps it is worth pausing to consider that little word 'our', so beloved by those who defend the status quo, and worth recalling Aneurin Bevan's book *In Place of Fear*, quoted in the last chapter, in which he describes the physical environment of Parliament as experienced by a newly elected Labour MP (bearing in mind that Parliament is opened constitutionally by the Queen reading 'The Queen's Speech'). Bevan recalls:

> His first impression is that he is in church... Here he is, a tribune of the people, coming to make his voice heard in the seats of power. Instead, it seems he is expected to worship; and the most conservative of all religions—ancestor worship... It is not the past of his people that extends in colourful pageantry before his eyes. They were shut out from all this; were forbidden to take part in the dramatic scenes depicted in these frescoes... the House of Commons is an elaborate conspiracy to prevent the real clash of opinion which exists outside from finding an appropriate echo within its walls. It is a social shock absorber placed between privilege and the pressure of popular discontent.

Moving to the left—so to speak—we find a vivid and amusing account by Trotsky of his first meeting with Lenin, then staying in rooms in the Tottenham Court Road; Lenin took the young Trotsky for a walk around London:

> From a bridge, Lenin pointed out Westminster and some other famous buildings. I don't remember the exact words he used, but what he conveyed was: 'This is their famous Westminster' and 'their' referred, of course, not to the English but to the ruling classes. This implication, which was not in the least emphasized... was always present... [T]hey know this or they have that, they have made this or achieved that...[1]

How fresh great political writing is—how little it seems to date! Do miners who saw their communities destroyed in the 1980s or single mothers on one of the 'sink' or 'dumping ground' estates really feel that the Queen represents *their* history? And if these examples seem too class-bound, here is the scientist and philosopher Jacob Bronowski, who lived in Britain from childhood:

> The men whom I have spent my life with have said little things on bits of paper, sometimes written in mathematics and sometimes written in poetry, which will shape the future of the

human race far more profoundly than those silly, political decisions. Power is very evanescent but knowledge is a tremendously compressed charge which waits for the future...[2]

We can think of quite a number of eminent scientists alive today who almost certainly hold a similar view of the history of the last sixty years, although they may be too polite to say so. In fact, the word *our*, when used in politics and political commentary, can be unusually seductive and insidious. Sadly, discussion of this fact is usually conducted in the *Daily Mail* or in rather abrasive and simple-minded left-wing writing. People like Sarah Bradford and James Munson seem to find it difficult to recognize that 'our' in this context properly refers to individuals like themselves. Those who are passionately fond of the monarchy are rather like football enthusiasts and the members of certain churches: they see life in terms of the objects of their adulation. But their terms of reference are likely to produce an incredulous or uncomfortable yawn in the rest of us.

Perhaps, after all, defending and justifying the existence of the monarchy is rather like arguing that the Earth is flat and that hellfire really exists; Mr Munson's intellectual contortions certainly suggest this, as when he quite rightly points out that British Prime Ministers have become increasingly American-style executive leaders, but goes on to add: 'In part this is because democracies like "strong leaders" — the twentieth century's greatest dictators were after all produced by democracies — and "strong government".' We cannot help wondering what kind of history Mr Munson has studied and feels that he has lived through and is currently living in — perhaps it is some kind of alternative history of which his Queen is the 'living representative'.

Mao Zedong was 'produced' by the overthrow of the Manchu dynasty in 1911 and the declaration of a republic that could not impose its authority on the Chinese warlords, followed by prolonged civil war and Japanese invasion, and then further civil war in which the communists prevailed after massive loss of life. Stalin was produced by a country that had known nothing but autocracy, and by the isolation of the

Bolshevik Revolution—intended by Lenin to be the first stage of a world revolution—in conditions of famine, economic collapse, civil war and the political disaster of Lenin's own death. Hitler's power sprang out of the humiliation of Germany by the Treaty of Versailles, worldwide recession, unemployment, the crucial backing of leading industrialists who saw him as their tool in crushing communism and the deep-seated anti-Semitism of central Europe. The democracy of the Weimar Republic had already largely crumbled when it gave in to Hitler through Hindenburg's appointment of the Nazi leader as Chancellor; even then, the Reichstag Fire was needed as the pretext for Hitler's abolition of the last vestiges of democracy. It was incipient civil war in Italy after February 1921, rioting in the major cities *and the fear of communist revolution on the part of the King of Italy, Victor Emmanuel III, who appointed Mussolini Prime Minister,* that 'produced' the first fascist dictator. And Mussolini never abolished the monarchy! The King of Italy presided over fascist excesses, including the murderous occupations of Ethiopia (Abyssinia) and Albania, becoming emperor and king of those unfortunate countries. As fear of dictatorship and the alleged role of the monarchy in forestalling it are major underpinnings of monarchist thinking, it is disturbing to find this eminent royalist writing about dictators with a blatant contempt for the facts that would make a *Pravda* journalist in the darkest days of Stalin blush.

In any consideration of the British monarchy we need to ask ourselves three questions. Is the influence of the present Queen and the heir to the throne a positive or negative one? Is the part played by the monarchy in British public life *as an institution* positive or negative? Is the *concept* of monarchy a valuable or a harmful one in the modern world? According to Mr Munson, the present Queen has 'done a great deal to enhance and maintain this country's standing in the world'. State visits and meetings with foreign leaders are given interminable attention and coverage.

Perhaps we could look at a different example. We recall that on the recommendation of the Colonial Secretary, Anthony

Greenwood, in November 1965, Harold Wilson urged the Queen to approve an order in the Privy Council detaching the Chagos Islands from Mauritius in order to hand them over to the Americans. The Queen did just that. Parliament was not informed. Almost exactly thirty-five years later, on 3 November 2000, the High Court declared the deportation of the islanders unlawful. But in June 2004 the Queen approved another order in the Privy Council that overturned the High Court judgement, pronouncing on the fate of thousands of her victimized, sold and oppressed subjects with one word: 'Agreed!'

Presumably, this is an example of the Queen's 'devotion to the Commonwealth', as James Munson calls it. Of course, monarchists argue that this kind of thing is not the Queen's fault because she can only act on the advice (instructions) of government ministers—an argument as easily deployed as the one that holds that she exercises an enormous influence for good in the country 'through carefully worded questions, advice and, rarely, warnings based on her long experience and independent position' (Munson again). No such questions, advice or warnings to help the Chagossians!

Further, James Munson proudly describes another example of the Queen's 'soft power'. A young man from Bristol wrote to the Queen asking for her opinion of the possibility of 'a blasphemous film about Christ' being made in Britain by a foreign director (the film is not specified). The Queen wrote to the young man to express her bitter opposition to the proposal, stating also that she had no objection to the publication of her letter. The film was not made. Naturally, it quite escapes the notice of religious people that nothing is 'blasphemous' in some absolute sense. Something can only be blasphemous *if* you are a member of a certain religious group, although non-believers may readily agree that some films, books or other works are tasteless and ugly.

In February 1989, people across the world were appalled when Ayatollah Khomeini condemned Salman Rushdie to death for his 'blasphemous' book *The Satanic Verses*. In a society that claims to take pluralistic democracy seriously there should be no such thing as a Church of England, still less the Church of Britain that is implied, but only the Anglican Church.

The Queen did not, of course, condemn anyone to death. However, we can imagine the uproar in the tabloid press and in serious papers and among serious people—and it would surely be justified—if a senior imam prevented an allegedly anti-Muslim film being made because he was 'bitterly opposed' to it. What if Arthur Scargill stopped the production of a film hostile to trade unions by his mere disapproval? Or can we imagine J.K. Rowling suppressing a film attacking single mothers through her publicly expressed resentment of its contents? Who can say, in any case, what the faithful may regard as blasphemous? *Monty Python's Life of Brian* was confidently labelled a blasphemous attack on Jesus Christ by people who did not take the trouble to watch it—if they had, they would have known that it was not about Jesus Christ. *Brian* was—among other things—a satirical attack on left-wing splinter groups and pedantic trade union officials, something that should have pleased those who denounced the film.

Moving from the Prince of Peace to the Prince of the Arms Industry, we find the heir to the throne imparting this piece of wisdom, standing near a hideous 'anti-personnel' weapon at the Dubai arms fair: 'The British are really rather good at making certain kinds of weapons. It's the hoary old chestnut. If we don't sell them, someone else will.'[3] The Prince seems at times to share the very shaky grasp of history from which his apologists suffer. A version of this argument is used to discourage many kinds of moral effort, including the banning of vivisection laboratories. Wilberforce, in his nineteen years of successful struggle to abolish the slave trade, was not deterred by the argument 'if we don't conduct this trade, someone else will'. It can also be argued—no doubt correctly—that the slave trade would have eventually disappeared as it became unprofitable, just as it can be said that Hitler's Nazi empire would have eventually disintegrated. Unfortunately, *eventually* can sometimes be a rather long time. It requires individuals prepared to make a moral effort together with objective conditions to bring about the next step in human progress—sooner rather than later. Apparently, the Prince is not prepared to use his influence to oppose the sale of devices that cause the agonizing deaths of children, just as his mother has failed to use hers to oppose the ethnic cleansing imposed on some of her subjects.

Individuals aside, we should consider the function of the British monarchy, which we are told 'reigns but does not rule', as part of the machinery of the state. John Pilger describes the way in which the Privy Council was twice used to violate the human rights of the Chagossians:

> [A] secretive, unaccountable group known as the Privy Council. The members of this body... include present and former government ministers. They appear before the Queen in Buckingham Palace, standing in a semi-circle around her, heads slightly bowed, like Druids... 'orders-in-council'—are read out by title only. There is no discussion; the Queen simply says 'Agreed'. This is government by fiat: the use of a royal decree by politicians who want to get away with something undemocratically. Most British people have never heard of it... prime ministers use it [for] unpopular wars... Egypt in 1956 and Iraq in 2003.[4]

Ex-cabinet minister Tony Benn made the point that: 'As colony after colony won its freedom... the British people found themselves virtually alone as subjects of the Crown.' He also points out that as late as 1977 the Central Office of Information in its annual handbook *Britain* described this country as a 'monarchical state', not as a parliamentary democracy. Benn continues:

> [D]e-colonisation [of the British people] might encounter opposition in a number of forms... the prerogatives of the Crown to dismiss and dissolve, and the loyalties of the courts and the services... might all be used to defend the status quo against the parliamentary majority elected to transform it... [T]hose forces opposed to democratic reforms could argue that they were operating in accordance with the letter of the constitution... Unlike countries where the overthrow of elected governments by a non-elected military elite... take[s] place... the British

Constitution *reserves all its ultimate safeguards for the non-elected elite*. (Emphasis added)[5]

The powers of the Privy Council—and by extension those of the Crown—were skilfully used by Margaret Thatcher during the war in the Falkland Islands. Let us remember that cabinet ministers are sworn into Her Majesty's Privy Council and sworn to secrecy by a personal oath made to the Clerk of the Council. Mrs Thatcher called for all-party talks on the crisis in the Falklands. Michael Foot, the Labour leader, refused. Such consultations would have been on 'Privy Council terms', which would have meant observing secrecy and thus curtailing the Opposition's opportunities to criticize the government. The Constitution was handily available to reserve the conduct of the war entirely to the Prime Minister, with the ready-made pretext that she had offered participation to other parties, or to muzzle effective criticism of her actions.[6]

Ultimately, the British Constitution and the monarchy do not guarantee democracy and safeguard against dictatorship at all. In a time of extreme crisis an opponent of the British government might be prosecuted and imprisoned under anti-terrorist legislation, something that has become far more possible since 11 September 2001. Even if this British Solzhenitsyn, Nelson Mandela or Aung San Suu Kyi (if one existed) had his/her conviction overturned by the High Court—more likely the High Court would declare the prosecution of certain *activities* to have no foundation in law—the Privy Council could be used to set aside the High Court judgement. And if this seems impossible, remember that the Britain of 2014 seemed impossible in 1964 or 1974.

Yet James Munson and those who share his views go on proceeding by argument-by-scare-stories. 'If the Queen did not open a new parliamentary session who would do so?', Mr Munson asks. 'Perhaps the duty could be vested in the Speakers or the Prime Minister of the day, invoking memories of the parliamentary dictatorship of the 1640s?' But why not invoke associations with democratic countries—our neighbours in Western Europe—that have no monarchy? Thanks to the powers of the monarchy, albeit quiescent ones, Britain is in a permanent state of inherent or potential dictatorship.

Finally, monarchy is based on a silly concept. Thomas Paine regarded a hereditary head of state as an absurd notion, quite as much as the idea of a hereditary physician or a hereditary astronomer would be. The idea that an individual should have the right to exercise enormous power, or influence and 'soft power', simply because he or she is born into a certain family belongs to the Middle Ages.

The continued existence of the monarchy is no more needed to provide 'legitimacy and historic continuity' (Munson) for the process of government than the continued use of public execution is needed to give legitimacy to the legal system, or the burning of heretics is necessary to legitimize religious life, or the idea of an Earth-centred universe is required to give continuity to astronomy and physics. (In the early twenty-first century, after over a hundred years, the conviction of thinkers such as Tolstoy, who believed that *nothing* gives legitimacy to the process of government, is once again growing in force and appeal.) However, monarchists go on insisting that a republic has to mean a republic on the model of the United States or France where the head of state is also the head of government; yet in Ireland and Iceland this is not the case, and the office of President of Finland has been scaled down in recent years to that of head of state rather than executive leader.

It would be perfectly possible to have a republic in which an elected president is not only the head of state standing above party politics, but also a person nominated as a candidate because of distinction in a non-political field who *must not be* a former minister or Prime Minister. Abolishing the monarchy does not need to mean transforming the office of Prime Minister into that of an American-style president. James Munson, pulling another spectre out of the bag, tells us that: 'Without Elizabeth II we would have President Blair or perhaps President Beckham [the footballer].' Presumably, this could also be updated to include President Cameron. This is as much nonsense as the assertion that 'the twentieth century's greatest dictators were after all produced by democracies'.

Why should we not have President J.K. Rowling, President Stephen Hawking (whose severe illness did not prevent public appearances and interviews for a number of years) or President Carol Ann Duffy? After all, the Czechs elected a creative writer as president. Even the grotesque prospect of President Beckham is hardly more dreadful than the actuality of Prime Minister Gordon Brown.

The concept underlying monarchy is infantile and infantilizing, especially when combined with the modern media-driven obsession with the Royal Family, quite as pernicious as soap operas and endless gossip about film stars, models and footballers. The scaled down monarchies of Norway, Sweden and Denmark exist in societies with deeply ingrained egalitarian and libertarian values, and so they are compatible with a highly educated and sophisticated electorate. Sadly, the monarchy in Britain reinforces the prejudices of the British and their inflated, insular and partly illusory notions of the strength of democracy in their country, as well as their lack of vigilance in matters of political freedom and their weak sense of historical awareness.

No serious republican movement of any size has existed in modern times, and even a debate over the continued existence of the monarchy forms no part of political life. James Munson loathes Tony Blair and admires the Queen — and presumably also Prince Charles — extravagantly. The essayist Christopher Hitchens loathes Prince Charles but admires Blair for his pro-Americanism. It is important to realize, however, that both Blair and Prince Charles are inimical to democracy, not because they are 'bad' human beings, which is largely an irrelevant issue, but due to their function and the role they have played and still play in the world. The continuing British acceptance of and enthusiasm for the monarchy suggests a crude proverbial injunction given to Victorian and Edwardian children, later adapted by Hilaire Belloc in a comic poem: 'Stick with Nurse, or you may find something worse.'

1. Edmund Wilson, *To the Finland Station*, New York, 1972; London, 1991 (previously, 1940, 1960, 1968).
2. Jacob Bronowski, *Journey Round a Twentieth Century Skull* (The last broadcasts), BBC Radio 3 and Radio 4 and the World Service; *The Listener*, 15 May–3 July 1975.
3. Interview with Jonathan Dimbleby, 'Charles, the Private Man, the Public Role', a Dimbleby Martin production for Central TV, broadcast 29 June 1994.
4. John Pilger, *Freedom Next Time*, London, 2006.
5. Tony Benn, *Arguments for Democracy*, London, 1981.
6. Stephen Blake and Andrew John, *Iron Lady: The Thatcher Years*, London, 2003, 2012, 2013.

Chapter Four

The Vacancy is Filled

Literature reflects the nature of the society in which it is written in at least two ways. The obvious way is by description and portrayal; we read a novel by Dickens or George Eliot (Mary Ann Evans) or Marx's *Das Kapital* and feel that we have to some extent *experienced vicariously* the reality of Victorian England, and that we are better informed about it. However, if a society does not produce writers who compose books that describe the social life around them, that also reflects the conditions of the times—we start to look for reasons for this. Are the writers of the day unusually timid? Is there a ferocious censorship? Is society so stodgy, comfortable and boring that creative writers do not find it an interesting subject?

J.B. Priestley has been largely forgotten as a novelist today, not entirely fairly; he did, however, write one book on literary history and criticism that is still useful today—*Literature and Western Man* (1960). Priestley makes the following perceptive comment on Hemingway: 'he could not draw on fresh life-giving resources of the spirit, nourishment from responsibility itself, from broadening experience... to settle down in or near any American city, take it in all over again, sink down some shafts, if necessary to find a new manner and forge a new style, and then write the great American novels of his maturity.' If we read 'British' for 'American', I suggest that something like this applies to the majority of writers in Britain since 1950, or certainly the novelists.

When I was in Sweden at Christmas 2003, I found something I had missed in Britain (apart from the way that public transport and all other traffic rolls on unperturbed despite a heavy fall of snow and a temperature of minus nine degrees): Swedish novels, including those promptly translated into English, quite often criticize and attack Swedish society. You only have to spend half an hour in any large bookshop in Britain to see that not one in twenty contemporary British novelists wishes to confront sickness and corruption in their own society *today*.

An article of mine called *When Poetry Keeps Faith and Fiction Does Not* was published in the excellent poetry magazine *Orbis* (number 131) that was founded in 1968. If I overstated my case in that piece, I did not overstate it by very much. Even such a distinguished novelist as Helen Dunmore writes—about what? Dunmore's *The Siege, House of Orphans, A Spell of Winter* are extraordinary books, and in them we find Leningrad in 1941, revolutionary Finland in 1901, forbidden, incestuous love... If we take Ms Dunmore together with a dozen gifted novelists, Jill Paton Walsh, Geraldine Brooks, Sarah Waters, Sebastian Faulks and others, we find splendid evocations of the French Resistance in the Second World War, the nineteenth-century music hall, D.H. Lawrence in Cornwall, the trenches of the First World War, Czechoslovakia before the fall of communism, the Great Plague. These are wonderful subjects and writers must go where their creative imaginations take them. Still, surveying literature in Britain from a distance, we cannot help being struck by the absence of CCTV surveillance, globalization, food banks, bailiffs, anti-terrorist legislation and climate change.

In short, how many British novelists are doing for Britain in the early twenty-first century what Tolstoy did for late Tsarist Russia in *Resurrection*, what Dreiser did for the United States of the early twentieth century in *An American Tragedy* and what Solzhenitsyn did for the Soviet Union of the mid-twentieth century in *Cancer Ward*? Indeed, how many writers have engaged with British society in this way since the Second World War?

Orwell presented a picture of Britain in his novel *Coming Up For Air*, and gave an even sharper and more comprehensive picture in the body of work that includes the novel and his non-fiction, *The Road to Wigan Pier*, *The Lion and the Unicorn* and *The English People*—a mature vision of society that has been almost unconsciously absorbed by conservative and right-wing people as well as those who share his outlook since his death, just as it provoked readers in his lifetime. Before Orwell, of course, there is a long line of writers whose work sprang out of indignation and moral concern with the state of society. Literature has always been a *moral activity*: it has been concerned with the difference between what human beings are and what they could be. This has always implied criticism of the social structure—there is a surprising amount of social criticism even in Homer.

However, the emphasis has changed through the ages; Judaeo-Christian literature dwelt upon humanity's place in a God-centred universe of moral imperatives, and the literature of the pagan ancient world presented the heroic loneliness of human beings in a world of capricious, cruel forces. The Renaissance shifted the focus of literature decisively to human beings and their aspirations and dignity. And then, from the seventeenth century—parallel with the Scientific Revolution—the moral endeavour that is inseparable from literature included an increasingly *conscious* awareness of society as a whole.

These profound changes affected all literature, even those literary works with grand religious themes; Milton's *Paradise Lost* (1667) is not much like the work of a convinced Christian poet of earlier ages, however much Milton might have wished it to be. (We should also bear in mind the fact that Milton's rousing defence of freedom of expression in *Areopagitica*, written in a time of civil war, still provides an answer to those who wish to suppress or prevent the production of works that offend their sensibilities, 'blasphemous' films included: 'He that can apprehend and consider vice with all her baits and seeming pleasures ... is the true warfaring Christian. I cannot praise a fugitive and cloistered virtue, unexercised and unbreathed, that never sallies out and seeks her adversary, but slinks out of the race... Give me the liberty to know, to utter, and to argue freely according to conscience, above all liberties.')

By the nineteenth century, of course, capitalism was fast evolving into a social and economic system more powerful and all-encompassing than any system in history; and the social dimension of literature was fully and firmly established. In novels, plays and much poetry there was an extra, unnamed character or figure, usually destructive or partly destructive — society itself. In non-fiction, intense passion over social and historical issues replaced religious fervour and ecstasy, and questions of meaning and truth, the stuff of philosophy, were to become interesting in as far as they had a social application and could be instruments of change.

The social dimension of literature has never disappeared since the nineteenth century, although the flame of social criticism sometimes burns very low. I suggest that the flame has burned particularly low in British literature since the Second World War, except in drama and some poetry. I think that here we come to an uncomfortable truth. Novels, documentary writing, polemics and books on history, together with screenplays, or plays that are filmed for television or the cinema, are the dominant literary forms in contemporary society. Stage plays and poems interest and affect only small minorities — this is a bitter but inescapable fact. Germaine Greer's *The Female Eunuch* changed attitudes and lives far more widely than the poems of Carol Ann Duffy ever have, however great the literary excellence of Duffy's poetry. An *Observer* review of Duffy's work stated: 'She deserves to outsell most of the novelists on your shelf.' Yes, Ms Duffy does deserve this, but it is not going to happen, even though she is perhaps the most admired and successful poet in Britain. It is absurd to think that any British, American or European poet today can ever have the influence that Anna Akhmatova had in Russia in her lifetime and for many years after her death. Even if a poet of the stature and radical passion of Shelley appeared in Britain today or in recent decades, his or her poems would have only a fraction of the impact of the books of John Pilger or even the historical works of Eric Hobsbawm, let alone the novels of Doris Lessing.

John Osborne's *Look Back in Anger* (1956) and the theatrical revolution it brought about appeared just within the fading echoes of the age of Ibsen and Shaw, an age in which stage plays really did shake society. But the impact of Osborne's play has also been increased by the 1958 cinema version and later television productions. The even angrier—and more intelligently indignant—plays of Caryl Churchill have not benefited from this kind of screen exposure. Therefore, a literature of healthy dissent and social concern in today's society depends upon novels and non-fiction books of literary excellence that are socially engaged; more broadly, commitment and social awareness in the arts depend also upon intelligent cinematic works. However superb poetry and drama may be today (actually, they are very rarely superb), however robust their defence of humane values and their defiance of injustice, they touch only tiny sections of the community.

A consideration of post-war British literature can usefully begin where Orwell left off. *Nineteen Eighty-Four* (1949) was the last novel Orwell happened to write, and *not* his last testament, something that Bernard Crick, the most intelligent of Orwell scholars, has repeatedly pointed out. Dystopian novels of any seriousness or worth are usually indictments of the present as well as warnings about the future; as such, Orwell's novel is a thoroughly intellectually consistent and self-explanatory projection of trends and dangers in the 1940s, but it is difficult to think of any other dystopian books written in Britain since the forties that approach Orwell's level of sophistication.

The division of the world into vast military-political blocs which are incapable of destroying one another and the increasing acceptance of a totalitarian outlook by the intelligentsia and by power elites in all industrialized countries formed the basis of Orwell's warning. The novel also makes it clear that there had been a limited nuclear attack on Britain around the year 1950, with an atomic bomb falling on Colchester, which may have been launched by the Soviet Union, but possibly by the United States; also, street fighting in London had followed, whether against an invading army or during a civil war. The details are uncertain because these events have occurred in the central character's early childhood and all records have since been destroyed.

Sadly, in the much weaker dystopian novels that have appeared since Orwell's book was published, events take place without adequate reason or explanation. Derek Raymond's *A State of Denmark* (1970) has a genuinely threatening mental atmosphere that sticks in the reader's imagination permanently, and it is brilliantly written, if uneven — descriptions of the exiled journalist-narrator's life in Italy are given too much space compared to the vivid depiction of a cruel, shabby, uncouth police state in Britain. But the reasons for Britain's descent into dictatorship do not extend much further than public apathy and the existence of a deceitful, unscrupulous and ambitious politician: there are always plenty of those! The Labour Prime Minister Jobling is presumably based on the worst characteristics of Harold Wilson — a 'falsely reassuring platitudinous voice', thick grey hair, bad teeth, a fat face and the pretence of coming from a working class background. It would take more than this to reduce Britain to *open* dictatorship, something not attempted by Margaret Thatcher or Tony Blair.

The Day of the Women by Pamela Kettle (1969) is engrossing, fast-paced and compelling, as well as a highly intelligent narrative of imaginary political conditions, but only after the reader accepts that the sequence of events described could begin at all. An all-female feminist political party is created and enters mainstream politics, winning a general election. The woman Prime Minister Diana Druce gradually establishes a dictatorship, carries out state murder of male children and introduces conception by artificial insemination without sexual intercourse on a wide scale (something occasionally suggested by lesbian separatist feminists in the 1980s). In the closing chapters she succumbs in rather conventional fashion to the paranoid delusions of many dictators. This has very little to do with the actual social revolution carried out by Mrs Thatcher, which was very much the result of a change of power within the Conservative Party and nothing to do with the election of a woman to the post of Prime Minister.

The new feminism of the sixties, seventies and eighties and the Women's Liberation movement at the peak of its influence were by their very nature anti-authoritarian, anti-government, anti-state and generally anti-capitalist. Mainstream women politicians were hardly ever radically feminist and radical feminists hardly ever entered mainstream politics. Some profound change in the consciousness of women would have had to occur in order to bring about this synthesis of opposites. No such change is described in Pamela Kettle's novel, and its necessity is simply ignored.

The famous novel *A Clockwork Orange* (1962) by Anthony Burgess is a moral fable that makes a worthwhile attack on the treason against human dignity and decency inherent in forcible mind conditioning — in this case by aversion therapy. However, the story depends on a projected dystopian and repressive future; it is made clear that the number of violent young offenders in prisons is to be reduced by the use of aversion therapy in order to make way for political prisoners. As in the novels by Derek Raymond and Pamela Kettle, no convincing sequence of events gives rise to this dictatorial order. The film version of *A Clockwork Orange* caused much predictable fluttering among the tabloid guardians of morality.

Burgess also concocted the ghastly, irresponsible and tasteless satire *1985* (published in 1978), which exhibited a shrill hysteria more typical of gutter journalism and gutter conservatives. The book appeared in the year before Mrs Thatcher's first election victory, an event which exposed its stupidity; even the trademark cleverness for which Burgess was famous had deserted him.

We need to look briefly at a work of fantasy, for reasons that I hope will become clear a little further on. J.R.R. Tolkien's *The Lord of the Rings* (1954–55) is aimed mainly at adults due to its length, complexity and sophistication of language, unlike its prequel *The Hobbit* (1937), which is manifestly a children's book.

Apparently, an opinion poll revealed that the majority of the British reading public regards *The Lord of the Rings* as 'the greatest novel of the twentieth century' — a verdict that requires no further comment.

The book is an epic synthesis of Norse, Germanic, Celtic and Finnish mythology, medieval romance and the most lurid aspects of Catholic theology. It is useful to look at it beside J.K. Rowling's *Harry Potter* series of fantasy novels, the early volumes of which are very much children's books, while the last volumes begin to cross into adult territory. Rowling somewhat overdoes the exploding-concoctions-and-farting-cushions side of her magical inventions; this aspect of the books jars somewhat and will date badly. However, the excruciating chapters of *The Lord of the Rings* set in the hobbit homeland, The Shire, grate on the twenty-first century reader with any taste far more than Rowling's laboured jokes, they are equivalent to Rupert Brooke's poem 'Grantchester' as described by Orwell, 'an enormous gush of "country" sentiment, a sort of accumulated vomit from a stomach stuffed with [English] place-names', they are also a vehicle for Tolkien's extremely unpleasant feudal beliefs.

Yet *Harry Potter* manages to encompass themes such as the bullying swinishness of respectable families, irresponsible popular journalism, the insanely authoritarian tendencies of bureaucracy and a horrified awareness of the evil of *self-corrupted* individuals, whereas Tolkien would have been quite incapable of writing of such things. Tolkien's Dark Lord, Sauron, is a version of the medieval Catholic Satan and is frequently called the Enemy (Satan means 'adversary' in Hebrew). Rowling's Dark Lord, Voldemort, was originally an ambitious, power-hungry youth who becomes evil through an utter lack of moral restraint. Tolkien was a very reactionary and old-fashioned Oxford philologist who could never have gone on to write a serious novel about contemporary society and would have hated the thought of doing so. But Joanne Kathleen Rowling went on to do just that.

The consistently left-wing Catholic novelist Graham Greene seemed to be a writer of Orwell's stature in the 1930s, as well as sharing many of Orwell's imaginative interests and passions. *The Confidential Agent* (1939) — about an agent of the Spanish Republicans in England — *It's a Battlefield* (1934) and *The Ministry of Fear* (1943) suggested, in the slick language that book reviewers would employ today, that Orwell had a serious rival. The Catholic fable *Brighton Rock* (1938), although its themes are spiritual and existential, evokes a good deal of the texture of Britain in those days. Significantly, Greene did not write novels about British society after the Second World War; and we cannot help wondering what excellent fiction he might have produced, for he is a writer of passion and compassion, perhaps the most serious and impressive *popular* novelist in twentieth-century English literature; his social background is somewhat similar to Orwell's, and he had an equally wide experience of the world. However, Greene is closer than Orwell to the profound and intelligent pessimism of Joseph Conrad.

J.B. Priestley's observations about Hemingway are uncannily apt in Greene's case: 'the style in the old sinister magical fashion, mastered him. It took him... to Africa, anywhere, in search of more violence, more death.' Admittedly, *The Power and the Glory* (1940), the story of a drunken Mexican priest hunted down by the revolutionary Mexican government, is magnificent. But *The Heart of the Matter* (1948) trivializes the story of Scobie, a Police Commissioner in a West African British colony, by ignoring the race issue and the problems of colonialism; while it is emotionally moving at first glance, the novel only serves as a vehicle for theological contortions that deceive the reader (and probably genuinely deceived Greene himself). An excessively kindly and humane Catholic convert like Scobie would not choose be a colonial policeman for years on end.

Some African writers have — quite unjustly, I believe — attacked Conrad's great novel *Heart of Darkness* (1899) for its 'petty European' focus, which seems to me the equivalent of condemning Shakespeare for not being a good democratic socialist. Greene wrote at a later date, when much greater awareness of the inner realities of racial oppression had become current; also, he had first-hand experience of colonial Africa; thus, one blushes at the thought of African readers coming across his character Scobie.

The Heart of the Matter deserved the vicious and deadly accurate review of it by Orwell: 'Hell is a sort of high-class night club, entry to which is reserved for Catholics only… when people really believed in Hell, they were not so fond of striking graceful attitudes on its brink.' It should be remembered that Orwell was also generous in his words about some of Greene's other books.

The series of novels with exotic settings, often impressive in themselves, followed over the long span of Greene's career. *The Human Factor* (1978) has a good deal of the old power, and convincingly shows the motivations of a British intelligence officer who is willing to work, to a limited extent, for Moscow: the Soviet Union *did*, despite its own ghastly faults, serve as a counterbalance to apartheid South Africa and the ineffectual opposition to the apartheid regime undertaken by the West, and the USSR often counterbalanced Western exploitation of the developing world. However, the British setting in this novel is only the background to the central character's secretive activities. Interestingly, we get in this novel what is probably Greene's own verdict on post-war Britain—rather small, commonplace, comfortable, 'a bit parish pump', which presumably explains the fact that he stopped writing novels about it. Mrs Thatcher did not think so, and the miners, her 'enemy within', could not afford to think so…

Greene's Catholicism sometimes undermined the balance and effectiveness of his art as a novelist, but not so consistently as communism does in the work of Edward Upward, whose trilogy of novels *The Spiral Ascent* (1962-1977) traces the story of a British communist from the 1930s to the 1960s and the struggles of CND, involving his rejection of the Party in the forties because of its Soviet-inspired betrayal of Marxism. These should be marvellous novels, but the ideological and propagandist tendencies are too rigid and the texture and style are too often drab; they have none of the insight and humour of Doris Lessing, who was once a communist. To support the Soviet Union less for what it was than for what it might have evolved into, to support it conditionally in a corrupt and predatory world, to see Stalin as an interesting, intelligent man, although murderously indifferent to human suffering, the product of the isolation of the Bolshevik Revolution, and perhaps as a necessity ('a useful man' as the German dramatist Bertolt Brecht called him), and to do these things with awareness and humour is quite compatible with being a good creative writer, whether we agree with that moral and political position or not. But to follow the party line dutifully and obediently *as a writer* and in thought as well as action is to produce rubbish, a mere mirror reflection of popular right-wing tabloid sentiments.

Two huge novel sequences cast a shadow over post-war British literature, Anthony Powell's *A Dance to the Music of Time* (1951–1976) and C.P. Snow's *Strangers and Brothers* (1940–1970). The literary historian Martin Seymour-Smith was at pains to defend Powell's sequence of novels as a great work of literature —and perhaps it is. Seymour-Smith reminds us that Powell conveys 'the sense of life as it actually passes before us... This is in fact reality. The passing of time is for once seen—without metaphysics or passion—as it is'. But *A Dance* cannot *also* give us 'a view of the whole of English life', as Seymour-Smith claims (*Guide to Modern World Literature*, 1985).

It is relevant to add that the viewpoint of Powell and his fictional narrator is emphatically aristocratic and upper class, though not 'snobbish', which has been unfairly asserted. Huge novels like *Middlemarch* and even *War and Peace* and James Joyce's highly innovative *Ulysses* depend upon selection in order to give us the sense, the impression, of an entire society. Novels like Proust's *In Search of Time Lost* and Powell's novel sequence also depend on selection (all literature and art does), but of a different kind. To convey the sense of life as it is actually lived and of time passing for the characters in Proust and Powell is different from creating the impression of an entire society living, working and interacting: they are different kinds of literary achievement. Proust's novel is full of 'society', but this is the landscape and scenery of the neurotic, sensitive narrator's past; it is not a society in the sense of those portrayed by Tolstoy and George Eliot and Dickens.

Less need be said of C.P. Snow and his novel sequence *Strangers and Brothers*. Snow studied physics at Cambridge, later coined the phrase 'the two cultures' to describe the mutual incomprehension with which scientists and literary intellectuals allegedly regard each other, and generally presented himself as a bridge between literature, science and politics—he was a civil servant and junior minister in the Labour government 1964 to 1966. But we only have to look at the rich variety of the work of Jacob Bronowski (1908–1974), scientist, scientific administrator, poet, philosopher, historian and dramatist, to see how shallow Snow's grasp of the scientific outlook really was. State enterprise, the 'classless', progressive public affairs of the sixties, government funded research, Cambridge and the business world form the environment into which Snow's fictional narrator climbs.

In the title of one of the novels in his sequence, *Corridors of Power* (1963), Snow added another fashionable and glib phrase to the language; and this one conveys the essential odiousness of his vision—the drab world of the men 'in the know' who run things for us, complacent, arrogant, completely unaware of their own pomposity and tediousness. Snow's creatures are still very much with us, inhabiting society like tapeworms in a human body, as full as ever of the nastiness that Snow never portrayed in his self-flattering books. For Macmillan, Wilson and Heath, C.P. Snow was a kind of Kipling of The Ministry of Social Security, without even a flicker of Kipling's vitality and colour. Prime Minister David Cameron has yet to acquire a Snow of The Department for Work and Pensions. But perhaps spectacular mediocrity is as unrepeatable as spectacular achievement. It is also likely that general political disillusionment is now strong enough to scald and wither a twenty-first-century Snow. To his great credit, Martin Seymour-Smith is particularly scathing about C.P. Snow, even if he may be too reverent about Anthony Powell.

Each of these writers, Greene, Upward, Powell and Snow, were born within two years of George Orwell, but outlived him by decades. It is extremely unlikely that the work of any of them will outlast Orwell's—only Greene and Powell are on Orwell's level, but Greene is ultimately less significant and impressive, while Powell will continue to appeal only to a minority, 'the cultivated circuit', smaller than the total readership of Proust.

Orwell will remain a permanent figure in British and Western culture along with Shakespeare, Swift and Dickens, writers he admired and did so much to celebrate. George Eliot (Mary Ann Evans), though less widely read, will also remain a permanent part of our culture because of her appeal to aware, independent-minded and educated women, as will Joseph Conrad on the strength of *Heart of Darkness* and his novels about terrorism, Russia and South America. It is simply implausible that more than two or three of the writers considered in the rest of this chapter will survive in this way, despite the extravagant claims made about some of them.

The Angry Young Men—the 'protest' novelists of the 1950s—were representatives of a mood rather than a movement; their anger was of 'far lower voltage' than the indignation of writers of previous generations and periods in literature, as the critic Gilbert Phelps pointed out; it did not indeed come near to the authentic intensity of John Osborne and his character Jimmy Porter in *Look Back in Anger*.

Jim Dixon in *Lucky Jim* (1954) by Kingsley Amis is a convincing creation in a genuinely funny novel that attacks academic pretensions and pomposities—a new generation of readers, especially young people who are entering academic life or know something of it, should rediscover this book. *Lucky Jim* is one of those books that define a period in cultural life, and it was enormously successful. Ultimately, however, the book, the author and that decade of writing do not amount to an awful lot.

Amis himself retreated increasingly into brittle right-wing indignation mixed with a genuine sense of humour; not that there is anything wrong with being right-wing or a comic novelist from a literary point of view. We can imagine a great novel—and a great comic novel—about twenty-first-century Britain being produced by someone of right-wing outlook, though not by a believing member of the Conservative Party. *Hurry on Down* (1954) by John Wain deals with a similar theme to that of *Lucky Jim*, but is very poorly written.

The 1950s also saw the appearance of a group of working class novels. *Room at the Top* (1957) by John Braine, film version 1959, enjoyed a certain notoriety for some years (presumably the supporters of Mrs Mary Whitehouse later prayed for Braine's divine punishment and were later still pleased that he had become a kindred spirit), but the novel is a crass piece of trash; Braine's hero—*not* anti-hero—Joe Lampton is the invention of a fundamentally stupid and vulgar mind, which becomes obvious as soon as we look at him beside Osborne's Jimmy Porter. It should be added, in fairness, that Braine impressively evokes the atmosphere of northern small-town life. We are left with the theme. Yes, strong-minded and gifted young men and women *do* frequently long to climb out of suffocating, grinding working class environments, and they sometimes do this by moral compromises, including rejecting a sexual partner they truly love in order to have a sexual relationship that brings material advantage. A good writer or a great writer would write a good or a great novel on this theme.

The most impressive portrayal of all would be the presentation of someone in Joe Lampton's situation from the inside, *just as he is*, without any moral preconceptions at all—but that would probably take a Shakespeare; not even George Eliot or Tolstoy in their own day could have quite pulled off that feat. But Braine does not show us a man in this situation just as he is. Instead, he gives us a piece of tough guy worship, written by an excited Yorkshire librarian who has heard just enough about something called literature to want to sit down and write a book, functioning in much the same way as a gangster thriller enthusiast who knows that gangsters are rather nasty people but admires them anyway. This point is worth elaborating, even though I am making it about a writer who has now been largely forgotten except by cultural historians—it applies to quite a large number of the 'important', 'significant', 'powerful' and 'uncompromising' films and novels that have appeared from the 1950s to the present.

It is refreshing to turn to Alan Sillitoe, another of the iconic working class novelists of the 1950s. All the novelists in this group suffer from narrowness of range and a rather slapdash style—this would presumably be true if John Braine and Stan Barstow, author of *A Kind of Loving* (1960) and *Ask Me Tomorrow* (1962), were good novelists rather than atrocious ones; Barstow is not nastily vulgar like Braine, but merely superficially realistic and astonishingly trivial.

However, these limitations do not matter in the case of Sillitoe. *The Loneliness of the Long Distance Runner* (1959) has an enormous power to move the reader—the young central character is a victim of the borstal (young offenders detention centre) system—it is an unrepeatable minor classic. *Saturday Night and Sunday Morning* (1958) is almost as good—a grim picture of harsh working class life enlivened by the energy of the book's anti-hero Arthur Seaton in thinking for himself; the story is even more convincing because Arthur is quite an unpleasant man.

Sillitoe has often been accused of writing his novels and stories to express his own emotional, simple-minded, anarchistic hatred of authority. What if he does? Some of us may feel that Britain would be a healthier place if more people had the same attitude. But apart from the question of how realistic Sillitoe's attitude actually is, the main thing is that the emotional attitude is the energy that fuels his work; and in the two works mentioned above he is sufficiently in control of his emotions achieve a great deal.

Finally, David Storey hardly belongs with the other working class novelists of the fifties and sixties or with the Angry Young Men because he is so much superior to any of them. Oddly, he does not seem to have received anything like the recognition he deserves, presumably because his novels are uncomfortable and difficult, dealing bravely and often shockingly with what might be called the conflict of body and soul. *This Sporting Life* (1960) is about a working class professional Rugby League player, a kind of modern gladiator, a celebrity in a spectator sport enjoyed for its violence. *Radcliffe* (1963) is a complex portrayal of a gay relationship written long before it was common to deal with that theme, all the more so because one of the men is working class and the other is upper class.

In the 1970s, when the attention of literary Britain was almost entirely focused on the late novels of Iris Murdoch, William Golding, John Fowles and Anthony Burgess, the publication of Storey's *Saville* (1976) had already taken place. This is a long account of a Yorkshire mining family and the rebellion of the young hero against parents who are decent and unselfish, but necessarily limited and constraining in their outlook. David Storey is a writer who has clearly absorbed the influence of European literature, as *Radcliffe* shows, contrasting with the pose of insularity and philistinism adopted by Amis and others. If a majority of readers in Britain really does regard Tolkien's *The Lord of the Rings* as 'the greatest novel of the twentieth century', then it is not surprising that the more aware minority usually prefers to be made to feel that it is getting its share of European culture by the likes of Murdoch, Fowles and Burgess than to get to grips with writers who really do draw inspiration from that tradition.

William Golding had the great virtue of being aloof from the literary trends of the 1950s, although his first three novels, *Lord of the Flies*, *The Inheritors* and *Pincher Martin*, all appeared within two years in the middle of the decade. *Lord of the Flies* is deservedly famous—the tale of the moral disintegration of a group of prep school boys who are stranded on a desert island during a nuclear war. The atmosphere is wonderfully created—all of Golding's first three novels pay painstaking attention to realistic physical detail—and the book can be read as a convincing account of the collapse of ordinary decency in an extreme situation and of the moving and heroic struggle of two boys to cling to sanity and humanity.

In this first novel we don't need to accept Golding's notion of the innate evil in human beings, and it does not intrude into the texture of the work. But in *The Inheritors* Golding is starting to manipulate his story and his readers in the interests of his own vision of the world; in this account of the peaceful Neanderthals being replaced by *homo sapiens*, there is no explanation of the murderous cruelty of the newcomers (ourselves). More coherent reconstructions of this period of prehistory were made in the novels of Jean M. Auel and Bjorn Kurten. After all, the evolution of human beings in groups in which members competed for food, status, sexual favours (like other primates) favoured the development of the capacity to imagine the feelings of others, and ultimately of compassion; greater and greater co-operation demanded an evolving concept of justice in order to balance the needs of the individual and the needs of the community; and thus these qualities were at least as essentially human as aggression and cruelty.

Human beings in the Palaeolithic era were not armed with a monotheistic religion such as Christianity, unlike white Europeans encountering Native Americans or Africans. Why would they see the Neanderthals as much different from themselves? In fact, it is overwhelmingly likely that the two groups found each other sexually acceptable. Golding can only explain the wilful viciousness of *homo sapiens* by his belief in innate human evil. It is all very well for a powerful writer in any *historical* period to incorporate such a belief into his/her work, but it is a serious flaw in a novel about the prehistoric beginnings of human society.

In *Pincher Martin*, the metaphysical message intrudes even further: we follow the struggles of a brave shipwrecked sailor clinging to a rock in the middle of the ocean in order to survive, reviewing his reprehensible past as he does so, only to discover in the last pages of the book that he has in fact drowned before he ever reached the rock and his ordeal was a spiritual experience in Purgatory.

However, *The Spire* (1964), a novel set in medieval times, is a magnificent achievement, not at all spoiled by Golding's preoccupations. We see in Golding another example of a highly gifted novelist finding his subjects—where? On a desert island, in Palaeolithic times, in the middle of the Atlantic ocean, in the fourteenth century… anywhere but in contemporary Britain, in fact.

Rites of Passage (1980) is set on a long sea voyage to Australia in the early nineteenth century and told in the first person; the narrative brilliantly recreates the historical period in which it is set, including the hateful and still feudal class divisions—vestiges of which still survive in Britain today and are considered normal and even a matter of pride by all too many people. One passenger, a young clergyman called Colley, has a sexual experience with a member of the crew (the lower class) when he gets drunk unintentionally; and the shame he feels kills him.

Intelligent critics have claimed that Talbot, the young narrator-hero, grows into maturity through realizing that he has failed in his responsibilities to Colley. This is not very plausible. Firstly, Talbot does make a decent effort to bring Colley out of his suicidal depression; secondly, the reader can see the part that hideous class divisions and class animosity have played in Colley's destruction, but Talbot is not shown as realizing this or changing his own class attitudes. The novel dwells upon the appalling spectacle of Colley willing himself to die and upon the vileness of the class system; Talbot's civilized regrets are rather peripheral and hardly life-changing.

Golding does deal with British society in *Darkness Visible* (1979), a grotesque and self-indulgent metaphysical concoction about innate evil and innate goodness that descends into passages reminiscent of a cheap political thriller. Matty has been disfigured as a young child in the Blitz, finds spiritual satisfaction in an antiquely printed Bible, and is finally responsible for the rescue of a child who will lead society to a new future. After leaving this life, Matty also summons a compulsive pederast schoolmaster to the next world and to freedom from the urges of physical life on earth. None of this has any genuine moral responsibility; it is, in fact, just clever inventiveness and brittle manipulation—a vehicle for the trivial nihilism of an overrated writer in decline. The seeds of that decline were in the first novel: the head of a slaughtered wild pig on a stick speaks, because a boy hallucinates, and the hallucination grows naturally out of the conditions on the island. Or does Beelzebub, Lord of the Flies, Satan's second-in-command, speak, turning the boys into his worshippers? In the first novel the reader has the freedom to take the story on a realistic level and appreciate the symbolism. Golding removes that freedom in his decline and becomes tedious.

The Roman Catholicism of Muriel Spark limits the world of her books far more drastically than Graham Greene is limited by his faith and far more than Golding's religious preoccupations influence his work. Indeed, for non-Catholics, Spark's world can sometimes seem almost as remote and strange in its own way as the world of a fantasy writer like Tolkien. She has had her devoted admirers and deserves them. Muriel Spark has a very small-scale talent beside Greene or Golding, but she usually writes with near perfection within narrow limits.

The Girls of Slender Means (1963) is set in the rather enclosed female world of a Kensington hostel in 1945, and involves turning to the religious life, grace and God working in mysterious ways, but is told with almost unremitting, sharp-edged humour. This strange book is another minor classic and will surely be continuously rediscovered and never long out of print. Spark is not, of course, taking literature or our understanding of the world anywhere (at least for non-Catholics, and probably not for Catholics either); she is a writer to be enjoyed and bypassed just as Tolkien is.

Far larger claims have been made for Iris Murdoch, as S.W. Dawson of Swansea University wrote in 1983, there was 'a thriving PhD industry in the unravelling and laying bare of mythic patterns in Miss Murdoch's work'.[1] Oddly enough, in a 1999 introduction to one of Murdoch's novels, Candia McWilliam refers to the author—who was made a DBE in 1987

—as 'Dame Iris' four times... a portrait of the young 'Dame Iris, child-faced', the titles in the list of Dame Iris's works, Dame Iris did make a study of 'frozen intellectual ingrates with dusty selfish ways' at Oxford, 'Dame Iris's descriptions of clothes'. How impressive! Quite what this is supposed to mean in a literary introduction that was intended to be taken seriously is difficult to say. Unwittingly, Candia McWilliam does catch the flavour of Iris Murdoch's work, in which she is constantly striving to impress, and in which she is therefore self-conscious and self-indulgent in the extreme.

It is interesting that Iris Murdoch published several books on philosophy and clearly regarded herself (quite justifiably) as a professional philosopher. For about three decades—inside and outside the academic world—Murdoch was seen as *the* intellectually demanding, heavyweight British novelist. She would not have made much of an impression in France, where philosophy is taken more seriously and novelist-philosophers really need to have intellectual weight, or be laughed at—as the careers of Sartre and Camus demonstrate.

Beyond the layer after layer of endless clues, symbols, displays of learning, descriptions of clothes, philosophy, psychology and anthropology, there is not the slightest indication in any of Murdoch's novels—many of them very long— that she writes with any genuine passion, anger or pity about anything. In *The Black Prince* (1973), one of her most highly regarded works, we have death (McWilliam calls it '*de facto* murder'), life imprisonment, cancer, with no sign that the author really cares about or has seriously imagined any of these things; she merely plays games and indulges in what Dawson calls 'contrivance' in his timely demolition of her pretensions.

This is novel writing on the level of all too many undergraduate philosophy seminars (I write from first-hand experience here): *Would you strangle a baby if by doing so you could ensure the permanent happiness of the human race?* There is nothing wrong with asking such questions in novels or in seminars, of course—but not as a clever little cerebral game. Apparently, Iris Murdoch was an interesting, intelligent and brave—if difficult

—person in her private life. But in case it is worth repeating, it should be emphasized that Murdoch's personal, private qualities are as irrelevant as those of Margaret Thatcher or John Braine; we are left with what individuals contribute to the society in which they live. Perhaps a fashionable reputation such as that of Iris Murdoch is a bad sign—several famous Russian writers have uttered remarks that are variations on the idea that approval is a terrible thing.

Margaret Drabble certainly seems to have acquired such a reputation, which probably distracts attention from her impressive achievements. It has been said that she has taken George Eliot (Mary Ann Evans) as a model, in which case she would have set herself the highest standards. In *The Millstone* (1965) an academic woman gets pregnant, finds in herself maternal feelings and discovers that this enlarges her sympathy with 'ordinary' women; it is of course an achievement for a novelist to make a story like this as moving as Drabble is able to do, but it is an even greater achievement that she avoids sentimentality. *The Ice Age* (1977) is an honourable and distinguished novel about corruption, greed and selfishness in Britain in the decade in which it was published. This book would be even more impressive if Margaret Drabble's characters were as convincing as—for example—Graham Greene's (except for the notable failure Scobie in *The Heart of the Matter*).

It is surely significant that one of the few truly great writers considered in this chapter grew up outside Britain and was 'not really English', although she came to be seen as so much part of the British literary scene—even by those who disliked her—that there came a time when you had to remind yourself that she had not been born in the UK or grown up in it. Doris Lessing grew up on a farm in Rhodesia (now Zimbabwe). Her anger at the treatment of the Africans made her a communist as a young woman—the same motivation as that of Graham Greene's fictional Soviet mole in *The Human Factor*.

Africa, racial issues and communism certainly play a significant part in her novel *The Golden Notebook* (1962), which, despite the fact that she regretted being always seen as the author of that work, is certainly her best book. This great novel is simply one of the best novels in English of the twentieth century; the award of the 2007 Nobel Prize for Literature to Lessing finally gave proper recognition to her stature and to that of *The Golden Notebook* particularly. Unlike that of some recipients of the Nobel Prize, Doris Lessing's award was as deserved as it was overdue.

The Golden Notebook begins in 1957; Anna Wulf writes in four notebooks of different colours, about her earlier experiences in Africa, about politics and communism, about her relationships with men, about her everyday life; in the golden notebook the strands are drawn together. Even this brief description would probably have made Doris Lessing uneasy; for she was saddened that readers saw only one book — the feminist novel or the book about left-wing politics or the book about mental breakdown. Lessing left communism behind and was impatient with the role of the great feminist writer, as Lisa Allardice wrote in *The Guardian* just after her death in November 2013, 'there are few political or cultural ideologies of the 20th century which Lessing did not embrace — only, usually, to divorce herself with equal ferocity'.

Although her changes of direction were abrupt and infuriating, they continued to inspire fine work. In *The Good Terrorist* (1985) she showed the aimless appetite for violence harboured by spoilt young middle class 'revolutionaries' in a suffocating and sinister London, in a book that can be mentioned in the same breath as Dostoyevsky and Conrad; and she does so without indulging in the trivial reactionary attitude that attributes such irresponsibility to *all* groups using violence and terror; her ghastly young 'revolutionaries' have been politely but firmly rebuffed by the IRA.

Doris Lessing was as infuriating, difficult, unwilling to remain at one stage of development — and as inspiring — as any great writer of modern times. Some of her readers (including myself) found her later science fiction novels mainly a disappointment, but she regarded them with more pride than any of her other works.

In the 1970s, when I was a young man, there was no doubt about which writers were the giants on the British literary scene or about whose new novels were greeted with the greatest excitement. Together with William Golding and Iris Murdoch, there were John Fowles and Anthony Burgess; Graham Greene was still grudgingly accorded a place alongside them because of his toughness, integrity and sheer durability, though he was not seen as very exciting anymore; Doris Lessing was still mainly for feminists and some other women, but had to be treated with a certain respect; every other British writer was a long way behind.

What taints them all in retrospect — except for Greene — is a cult of cleverness; yet this was much harder to see at the time. Fowles deserved much of the attention he got because of his novel *The Magus* (1966, revised 1977), a book in which his appetite for ingenuity and cleverness works with the grain of the story and is not merely self-indulgent; also, the sheer energy and momentum of the novel carry it forward; there is also the fact that some of its subject matter — including Nazi atrocities in Greece — demand a certain dignity and seriousness; with a larger measure of energy and seriousness the novel might have attained greatness. Nonetheless, this book about a young Englishman on a Greek island who finds reality being manipulated around him by the intelligent, enigmatic millionaire Maurice Conchis is a formidable work.

Sadly, this was followed by *The French Lieutenant's Woman* (1969), which is an irritatingly pretentious piece of arch cleverness, a pastiche of a solid Victorian novel with intrusions by the author reminding us that it is only a novel after all; with a detachable essay on Victorian sexuality and documentary additions and alternative endings included; much of this was inspired by the *nouveau roman* ('new novel') in France, a movement that sharpened awareness but did not really take literature anywhere — and all of this removed any interest in a story that was hardly compelling in the first place. It was actually enjoyed as a piece of slack literary-philosophical criticism by people who wanted to be reassured that they were right there at the sharp end of the latest cultural thinking.

Fowles gave the impression of a writer in whom creative pressure had been switched off by abundant success. He did not take himself as seriously in his games as Iris Murdoch and so was considerably wittier, as well as (just about) avoiding the fundamentally irresponsible callousness of her books or of Golding's *Darkness Visible*. Fowles returned to serious novel writing with *Daniel Martin* (1977), which presumably had elements of autobiography—there are a number of resemblances between the careers of Fowles and Daniel. But in this novel, too, the voice of Fowles, not Daniel's voice, can be heard —so to speak—too often murmuring in the background: I am a great novelist and just see where I take this novel! However, *Daniel Martin* is a rewarding book, even if it is rather too much concerned with the privileged, Oxford educated elite. The milieu can be a distinct drawback; a political passage that shows some prescience about the coming 1980s and considerable insight into the Conservative and conservative mind is rather blunted by the fact that it is only a comfortable after dinner conversation; also, Fowles chooses a fairly intelligent and realistic Conservative, but he is not an impressive or particularly interesting man, not honourable or vicious. There is a beautiful evocation of Daniel's boyhood, drawing a fascinating personal connection with Daniel's adulthood—the novel would be on an altogether higher level if we were shown the connection between that time and the 1970s.

Anthony Burgess (another Catholic writer) was made even more famous by Stanley Kubrick's 1971 film version of his fable *A Clockwork Orange* published nine years earlier, both film and book were worthy enough as moral indictments of mind control; yet it is easy to see how much the book relied on the clever use of slick techniques, including a piece of mind conditioning in the text itself—the repeated use of Russian words as the gang world slang of the youthful characters leaves the reader knowing a small Russian vocabulary by the end of the story, irresistibly and without conscious effort.

This tendency grew ever stronger in the novels of Burgess, except for *1985*, considered earlier as a dystopian novel, which is merely tasteless, irresponsible, shrill and silly. The cleverness was brittle, frigid and endless, as in *MF* (the anthropology of Levi-Strauss in a novel, and guess what? The hero is a black guy after all!); *Beard's Roman Women* (this is how women gang rape a man); *Earthly Powers* (the autobiography of a gay man born in the late nineteenth century who is also a very mediocre writer, through the First World War, the Paris of James Joyce and Hemingway in the 1920s, the Nazi Holocaust, contemporary America and arriving at the same innate human evil that Golding goes in for, but without a disfigured, outcast character to display innate goodness). We are perfectly entitled to ask just what evidence there is that *in the act of writing* (kindly personal qualities apart) Burgess cared in the slightest about any of this, just as we can ask the same question about Iris Murdoch. His cleverness is cleverer than that of Murdoch and better integrated into his tales, and he is a better spinner of yarns, but this fact hardly reflects well on either of them.

In *The History Man* (1975) by Malcolm Bradbury — a writer who still loomed large on the literary scene until quite recently — we get a very different kind of anti-hero in the academic world from Amis's *Lucky Jim*. Bradbury's Howard Kirk is a left-wing, 'new university' sociologist, and since Bradbury's hatred of Marxists in his books is a literary reflection of what became the vacuous and limp Social Democratic Party a few years later (as Martin Seymour-Smith astutely pointed out at considerable length), Kirk is damned on all counts, naturally a manipulative and dishonest swine.

Bradbury was to continue in the same vein in *Rates of Exchange* (1983), a tired and stale comedy about an academic visit to Eastern Europe, which tells us nothing about the Soviet Union and the Eastern bloc; he might have taken the trouble to read or to learn from Solzhenitsyn's memoir *The Oak and the Calf*, which, despite the author's view of himself as lone anti-communist crusader and saviour of Russia, is really very funny indeed in places and has many insights into Soviet life.

We return to the present in considering Graham Joyce, a writer who has probably not received the recognition he deserves because his work is set on the boundaries between fantasy and harsh realism. In fact, Joyce occupies the same imaginative territory as the Swedish writer Majgull Axelsson in her *April Witch* (1997, English translation 2002), one of the books that most impressed me for engaging critically with Swedish society. Joyce's *Some Kind of Fairy Tale* (2012) uses the main character's twenty-year absence in a magical world to put present day Britain and the Britain of two decades before into perspective. He confronts subjects such as the seeming near-inevitability of police corruption, the leaden weight of mass living habits and the legalized brutality of the psychiatric system which victimizes women most of all.

The Limits of Enchantment (2005), set in the mid-sixties, is richer and more detailed. Hopefully, Graham Joyce will choose a still larger canvas, a novel on the scale of *April Witch*; he remains a writer of huge potential.

The survey of British literature since the Second World War given so far in this chapter is not, of course, exhaustive. Quite a number of writers have been left out, for varying reasons, and many readers will be able to think of novelists who go against the trend and pattern I have described. Still, I don't think I have given an unfair picture of the creative writing of the period, which is in fact mostly within my own lifetime. Mainly, this is how the British have portrayed their society to themselves and to the world — or failed to portray it at all. It is far from a reassuring or inspiring survey. Why has British literature declined? Why does one of the most eminent novelists to write about Britain come from outside it, from Rhodesia, now Zimbabwe? Surely because Doris Lessing grew up in a society in which there was inequality and tyranny far worse than in Britain even in the darkest days of the 1930s, and she was therefore shaped by that experience. Martin Dodsworth points to a failure of confidence on the part of British writers when confronted with literature in other parts of the world since the war (in *An Outline of English Literature*, edited by Pat Rogers, 1998):

> Since the fifties the novel has been especially strong in America (Nabokov, Bellow, Malamud, Bashevis Singer) and Russia (Pasternak, Solzhenitsyn, Sinyavsky). In the late sixties Latin America joined them... The result was a sapping of confidence, a flight from large themes... Nadine Gordimer, Doris Lessing and V.S. Naipaul represented, by their talent, a new threat.

In 2012, some years after the almost unbelievable worldwide success of the *Harry Potter* children's books, J.K. Rowling's first novel for adults, *The Casual Vacancy*, was published; it marked about as complete a break as could be imagined from the series of children's books, which might be seen as an act of considerable nerve and courage. It is easy to say that Rowling could *afford* to be brave, but this assumes that a writer cares first and foremost about financial success, which—above the level of purveyors of various kinds of pulp fiction—is not the case. There is no reason to suppose that the atrociously bad writer John Braine, or the pompous C.P. Snow, whose 'message' is inimical to ordinary decency and intelligence, would ever have written differently just in order to make more money.

Be that as it may, Rowling made the transition from the world's most successful children's writer and everyone's favourite Mum to harsh social realist. The hype and general fuss preceding the publication of the novel was enormous and was easy to make fun of—some of the author's admirers as well as her detractors did this, and with some justification. But this is just the way that publicity and marketing work, particularly with a writer of Rowling's earning power: publishers who have made millions expect to make millions more.

Regarding the novel itself, one fundamental point should be made at once. *The Casual Vacancy* is an angry, even furious, and intelligent attack on some aspects of contemporary Britain—everyone, even the bitterest opponents of the novel, agreed on this. Next, here are some quotations from reviews: 'future generations will read it with wonder and awe', 'the tone of this huge book that is so marvellously new... a loud laugh is more crushing than a howl of agony', 'there has been no such analysis of the corrupting power of the police state', 'A chilling and truthful vision of women's precarious position', 'A dazzling performance that will make the blood run cold', 'A brilliant, deadly book'.

However, these quotations are *not* taken from reviews of *The Casual Vacancy*. The first three excerpts are from reviews of novels about the Soviet Union by Alexander Solzhenitsyn, who won the Nobel Prize for Literature in 1970, and the other three are from reviews of novels about Austria by Elfriede Jelinek, who won the Nobel Prize in 2004. Both these writers indignantly and bitterly attacked the societies in which they lived and in which they had grown up. And if a similar novel was written about Putin's Russia today and translated into English, it would be greeted with similar respect and praise. The French, of course, have continuously attacked every aspect of their own country and hardly ever stopped fighting among themselves for the last two or three hundred years. The novels that are written by Finnish and Swedish writers showing a deep discontent with their countries are not very suitable as partisan ammunition because the Scandinavian countries are barely noticed in Britain. However, we can be quite certain that a German writer who attacked Merkel's Germany would become the idol of the people who deeply resented Rowling's book. And best of all would be a book that angrily 'exposed' the faults of Muslim communities written by a Muslim.

In case it is thought that I am taking an over-sensitive and excessively polarized view of the argument over *The Casual Vacancy*, it is worth remembering the description of the novel by Jan Moir in the *Daily Mail* on 27 September 2012: 'more than 500 pages of relentless socialist manifesto masquerading as literature.' The insistence upon seeing this or that book as 'on my side' or 'siding with the enemy' does indeed degrade literature, but it is a consideration that middle England, the popular press and politicians take very seriously. There is probably a considerable, partly submerged, feeling of betrayal in the attitude to J.K. Rowling on the part of many right-wing and conservative people, even some of the most intelligent ones. Here is a writer who became extremely rich and reaped all the rewards of the capitalist system, was accepted by the establishment (except for some Christian fundamentalists, mostly in America) and was awarded an OBE—and what does she do? She writes *The Casual Vacancy*! Of course, she once lived on benefits and was a single mother who wrote in cafes, which just goes to show that you can't trust these people! A similar feeling of betrayal was felt towards Tony Benn and towards Jane Fonda in America.

Whatever else it may be, *The Casual Vacancy* is not a 'socialist manifesto', any more than Dickens was a follower of Karl Marx. The popular press is not notable for clarity of thought and precision of language, but it ought to be fairly well-known that any political manifesto does two things in quick succession: it exposes a problem and suggests a political solution that will solve the problem. Rowling's novel does the first thing (though this is a considerable over-simplification) but it certainly does not do the second.

Ultimately, Rowling, like Dickens, is attacking 'an expression on the human face', as G.K. Chesterton put it. The expression is always with us, but it takes on different forms and variations at different times in history and in different places. It is almost impossible to imagine literature—except for celebrations of joy, ecstasy and love—that did not attack that 'expression on the human face' in one way or another, and certainly impossible to imagine serious novels that failed to do so.

What is impressive about *The Casual Vacancy* is that it directs its attack at British society now, and does so with a range and breadth and seriousness and intelligence that have been as frequently absent as the willingness to engage with the social realities around us. Significantly, J.K. Rowling gets away from intellectuals or 'exceptional' people of any kind in this book, which even Doris Lessing in *The Golden Notebook* did not do. There were reviews of Rowling's book as enthusiastic as the ones written about the novels of Solzhenitsyn and Jelinek from which I quoted above. But even some of those who praised the novel pointed out that Rowling's prose style is not distinguished and she has a tendency to lapse into clichés. What if it isn't? The writing styles of Dostoyevsky, Theodore Dreiser, Jack London and George Orwell in *Nineteen Eighty-Four* have been found similarly disappointing, while that of Graham Greene is often far from graceful. Further, 'sliced through his brain like a demolition ball' — for instance — is not a cliché, just a rather poor simile, and 'funny and tough; impossible to intimidate; always coming out fighting' is the reported thought of one of the characters and entirely appropriate in its context.

The Casual Vacancy tells the story of the events that follow the death in office of a local councillor, Barry Fairbrother, in the 'idyllic' village of Pagford in the West of England, the inhabitants of which hate and fear the nearby council estate, The Fields, a place where most of the tenants live on benefits and in which there is widespread drug addiction. Fairbrother had grown up in The Fields; he was a decent man who struggled for the wider social inclusion of adolescents from the estate, including the notorious Krystal Weedon, a girl whose mother is a prostitute and a heroin addict. He includes Krystal in the rowing team he organizes at the local comprehensive school. Thus, Barry Fairbrother is the only adult who has believed that Krystal is worth anything and can achieve anything; later it turns out that the success of the rowing team — their ability to believe in themselves as a team — is largely made possible by Krystal. The middle class inhabitants of Pagford wish to shift the responsibility for The Fields to a neighbouring council: if they can elect the right kind of person to Fairbrother's vacant seat they can secure the necessary majority to do this.

The novel portrays a wide range of characters — including Krystal herself; the council leader and delicatessen owner Howard Mollison and his wife Shirley; Parminder Jawanda, a local GP and her family; Mollison's son Miles and his wife Samantha; Krystal's mother Terri; the social worker Kay; the printer Simon, a violent, controlling father, and his son Andrew. There is also Stuart, 'Fats', the teenage son of a local school teacher.

About halfway through reading *The Casual Vacancy*, I did something I had never done before when reading a novel: I made a list of all the characters and assessed them morally. I found all of them lacked any human decency, or were insipid, except for Krystal, and of course Barry Fairbrother who dies on the third page. But this is not how they are shown by the end of the novel, or at least not all of them. Thus, the reader is unwillingly made to share the fear, blanket condemnation and defensive objectification that the middle class residents of Pagford employ towards the people who live in The Fields. Further, Rowling convincingly shows us the world of the novel as a microcosm of Britain. The attitude of the people of Pagford is mirrored in the view taken by government ministers and politicians and the people who support them towards the underprivileged, disadvantaged and impoverished members of society, seeing them as an undifferentiated mass to be dealt with by this or that measure. However, those reviewers and readers of the novel who saw *all* of the characters, middle class or from the council estate, as 'horrible' or mentally and morally 'dead' were either mistaken or did not read the book to the end.

Whether she does so merely intuitively or entirely consciously, J.K. Rowling understands the anthropological function of fear of the underclass in a bourgeois community; firstly, there is the sense of physical threat and of contamination and a resentment of those who (allegedly) do no work and (allegedly) live at 'our' expense; but also The Fields (and generally in society — the unemployed, benefit cheats, asylum seekers, drug addicts, the disabled) represents the externalized bad conscience of respectable citizens about their own behaviour. The heroin addiction of Krystal's mother mirrors the compulsive overeating of the grossly overweight Howard Mollison. This is made dramatically explicit when Parminder, his GP, tells Mollison exactly that in public. Krystal's uninhibited sexuality enacts the longing to have sex with adolescent boys that preoccupies Samantha, the sexually frustrated middle class wife.

All of the characters — except those who are simply overwhelmed as victims — have serious moral faults and failings;

even Fairbrother is resented by his widow Mary because so much of his attention was taken up by his devotion to the community. Parminder, despite her decency and integrity, is coldly indifferent to her tormented daughter Sukhvinder to a near-fatal extent. However, Stuart Wall, 'Fats', son of the despised deputy head of the comprehensive school, seems to be altogether in a different dimension—a figure out of Dostoyevsky or French existentialism, intelligently dedicated to living authentically, which means in his case a dedication to cruelty and evil, including the methodical persecution of Sukhvinder, driving her almost to suicide. And Howard Mollison and his wife Shirley are creatures far worse than any reviewer of the novel seems to have recognized; not merely 'pompous' as it has been said, not merely full of petty, small-minded, middle class spite, but individuals beyond all hope of regeneration or change or redemption. Like The Fields drug dealer and rapist Obbo, the Mollisons have become irretrievably evil by their own actions over a lifetime; no flicker of awareness of their real selves will ever again pass through their minds; they are the real human counterparts of the monsters of Rowling's fantasy fiction.

Evil is not cosmic and external or 'innate'; it is generated by choice and deliberate action. Shirley is about to murder Howard because she fears public humiliation when it is revealed that he has been unfaithful years before. Actually, she finds him in the throes of a severe heart attack when she is about to do the deed. But she never acknowledges her intention to herself and it never lessens the venom of her self-righteousness. Previously, the stink of moist, infected flesh in the folds of Howard's massively bloated body stands for his moral putrescence—the details of his medical state have been described so carefully that this does not appear as contrived.

Like Solzhenitsyn's *Cancer Ward*, Rowling's novel is one of those books that work perfectly on the realistic and on the symbolic level. Barry *Fairbrother* dies, and the action stems from that event. 'Fair' means both beautiful in the old-fashioned use of the word as well as meaning right and just—the quality upon which the British have always most prided themselves; while *brotherhood* implies not only equality, but also a sense of community and responsibility to others. This is Britain when those qualities are in danger of dying.

The death of Robbie, Krystal's infant brother to whom she is fiercely and utterly devoted, is the sacrifice of the innocent that is a catalyst for change and regeneration in several of the characters. Krystal blames herself and commits suicide in an act of almost pagan nobility and despair. 'Fats' too is shaken by his share of the responsibility for the little boy's death, and draws back from his cultivation of evil; only his father, the school teacher crippled by severe obsessive-compulsive disorder and despised by everyone, shows him compassion; and father and son reach towards a new understanding. Sukhvinder bravely tries to save Robbie from drowning, an act that not only brings her the acceptance and respect she has never had, but also alerts her mother to the suicidal state she has reached. Samantha is plagued by guilt over the fact that she might have saved Robbie, which creates a new sympathy between herself and her husband (we wonder in this case how long the change will last).

In *Daniel Martin* by John Fowles, a good book in itself but without anything like the stature of *The Casual Vacancy*, an intelligent middle class woman says that if Russia needs a Solzhenitsyn, then Britain needs one too. This chapter has been mainly dedicated to that proposition. It is possible that such a writer has now appeared. Time will show us whether the vacancy has really been filled.

[1] S.W. Dawson, 'Iris Murdoch: The Limits of Contrivance', in *The New Pelican Guide to English Literature, Volume 8: The Present*, edited by Boris Ford, Harmondsworth, 1983.

Chapter Five

The Spaniard, the Brazilian, the Russian and the German

The British Foreign Secretary William Hague was answering questions in the House of Commons early in September 2013 — the subject was Gibraltar. In the July, Spain had reacted to the Gibraltar government's decision to lay seventy-four concrete blocks on the seabed off the coast, which impeded Spanish fishing. New restrictions were imposed at the border with Gibraltar. Mr Ian Paisley Jr. rose to his feet and said: 'Can I make it abundantly clear to the Spanish that if they continue their hostility to the people of Gibraltar, that you [Mr Hague] will tell the ambassador here in London to pack his sombrero, straw donkey and sangria and go?' Hague met the suggestion with an indulgent smile and the rejoinder, 'I think, if you'll forgive me, we will use slightly more diplomatic language'. The exchange was reported approvingly, but, it must be said, fairly and accurately by the *Daily Express*.[1]

As someone with a deep affection for Spain and the Spanish, who lived for most of two years within sight of Gibraltar, I must point out that I don't think that Spain has the slightest moral claim to the territory. Spain has two colonies on the mainland of Morocco, Ceuta, which can be seen from Gibraltar, and Melilla. Helen Wade, a bilingual journalist who grew up in Gibraltar, published a sane and good-humoured article on the subject in the *New Statesman* of March/April 2014, with which I happily concur; I would only dissent from her claim that it took twenty years after Spain fully reopened the border in 1985 for Spanish-Gibraltarian relations to thaw.

When I lived in southern Spain in the early 1990s, I found that the Spanish accepted Gibraltar just as they accepted the British exiles living alongside them (including, temporarily, myself). Jealous emotions over sovereignty were for the politicians to indulge in. The significant fact is that Paisley's choice of words caused no stir and no objection; if, on the other hand, he had used demeaning stereotypes when referring to the diplomatic representative of India or of an African country, he would have been regarded with disgust, and quite rightly so.

Forty years of membership of the community of Europe seem to have taught a large section of the British public and most British politicians nothing at all, except to be even more insular and anti-European or to defer to anti-European sentiments. Paisley's words fell on fertile ground in a country in which the current Prime Minister promises a referendum on leaving Europe and lives in fear of the anti-European right wing of his party and of the UK Independence Party. The grotesque pressure group UKIP is able to wield power vastly beyond its size and status because of the fears of mainstream politicians that it will attract the support of disgruntled voters.

It had long been predicted that UKIP would perform extremely well in the local and European elections of 2014, and that is exactly what happened. Of course, in any foreseeable political conditions, UKIP will never be a serious electoral force; support for this party will peak (or has already peaked); the greatest imaginable UKIP success would be a handful of Westminster MPs. As I write, the total is two.

In *The Road to Wigan Pier*, Orwell warned of 'a slimy Anglicized form of Fascism, with cultured policemen instead of Nazi gorillas and the lion and the unicorn instead of the swastika'. This is a partially accurate description of UKIP—the real nature of the party and its appeal was demonstrated by the incautious remarks of some of its members who were unable to keep their mouths shut and were then expelled for their lack of self-control. Sadly, the deep-seated racism of which UKIP is a symptom will prove to be far more enduring.

This anti-European group has made British xenophobia more acceptable, so that mainstream politicians who lack nerve and integrity feel that they have to compromise with these prejudices. This process is likely to accelerate if Britain leaves the European Union; in a Britain outside Europe, racism — especially anti-European and anti-Muslim — will become acceptable and normal. A Britain-for-the-British attitude may become as fundamental and expected as 'anti-communism' used to be in American life. Leaving the EU would be a far worse fate for the British than for most European societies. New leaders of the Thatcher and Blair type, armed with an even nastier British chauvinism, would thrive in that atmosphere.

Back in the same month of September 2013, Raquel Rolnik, a UN inspector with responsibility for the human right to housing, visited the UK to investigate the government's 'spare room subsidy' or 'bedroom tax'. Miss Rolnik recommended that the bedroom tax should be abolished as an abuse of human rights:

> The right to housing is not about a roof anywhere, at any cost, without any social ties. It is not about reshuffling people according to a snapshot of the number of bedrooms at a given night. It is about enabling environments for people to maintain their family and community bonds, their local schools, work places and health services,... education, work, food and health.

The Coalition government, in which the Liberals had compliantly accepted the bedroom tax, was already highly sensitive on this issue. It must be said, in fairness, that the *Mailonline* article by Matt Chorley was pro-government but reasonably even-handed. The Conservative Party chairman Grant Shapps was furious: 'It is pretty outrageous... Who invited her?' (We might wonder if UN inspectors need an invitation to look at conditions in a member state. Isn't it only our enemies who try to keep them out in order to conceal their ill deeds?)

The Conservative MP for Peterborough, Stewart Jackson, called Miss Rolnik a 'loopy Brazilian leftie'. No doubt the refusal by Hans Blix, the UN weapons inspector in Iraq, to endorse the claims by Bush and Blair that Saddam Hussein had Weapons of Mass Destruction had left painful memories. Clearly, the UN was only to be accorded any credibility or respect when it supported the point of view of the British establishment. All this was pretty predictable, except that it demonstrated that the fact that Miss Rolnik was a representative of the UN, a foreigner and a Brazilian was as offensive as her condemnation of the bedroom tax.[2] It was yet another ugly feature in the deepening atmosphere of xenophobia in Britain today.

The bedroom tax itself is certainly more oppressive and cruel than Mrs Thatcher's poll tax, although it has not been met with protests on the mass scale of those directed at the poll tax. It shows vividly how irreversible Mrs Thatcher's revolution in attitudes and outlook really is; for without that revolution it would not have been conceived, executed and found broadly acceptable; the same must also be said of the existence of ATOS and its obscene treatment of the sick and disabled during 'work capability assessments', although these measures do seem to have been defeated by public disgust and a handful of brave individuals.

The justification for the bedroom tax is the saving of some £500 million every year. Tenants in social housing have 14% of their housing benefit cut if they have a spare bedroom and 25% cut if they have two or more spare bedrooms; the idea is to force them out into smaller homes. The conditions on which housing benefit is paid and the checks carried out are very stringent, most of all for those paid total housing benefit to cover their entire rent; thus those affected are already defined by law as the poorest members of society; unable to make up the shortfall caused by the loss in housing benefit, they fall further into arrears and debt, risking eviction. Overwhelmingly, they live in a house with a spare bedroom because this was the size of the home originally offered to them by councils and housing associations, before the bedroom tax was envisaged, or because their children have grown up and moved out.

Quite apart from pushing people into accommodation away from their friends, families, communities and the rest of the social network that Raquel Rolnik referred to, or denying them the natural right to a spare room for a guest or for grown up children when they come to visit—we need only think of the typical size of the homes of the politicians who invented this law—the stock of available smaller homes is not large enough. Therefore, the victims often have no choice except to stay where they are in debt. On 29 March 2014, *The Independent/i* reported BBC research that revealed that only 6% of the tenants affected had in fact moved home. A report commissioned by the Department for Work and Pensions itself, published on 15 July 2014, presented an even more damning account of debt and 'heat or eat' hardship for those affected.

The supporting 'moral' argument for the bedroom tax goes as follows. How can it be moral for some families to occupy houses too large for them and get their rent paid when some families are forced to live in accommodation that is far too small? The answer is that it is not moral at all for people to be forced to live in homes that are too small for their needs. It is also not moral to address that problem by making other disadvantaged people suffer. The Thatcherite view of the poorest members of society as an inert, undifferentiated mass to be shifted in this or that direction according to expediency and policy has reached new depths after Margaret Thatcher's death. After the seemingly permanent advances of the decades that followed the Second World War, this development is a surprising twist of history. This is a point worth emphasizing: Britain, with its ill will directed outwards towards other nations and inwards towards its own citizens, presents the spectacle of a disagreeable society—I use the mildest possible term.

The instability in Ukraine increased as the spring and summer of 2014 advanced, perhaps with serious and unknown consequences... I wrote the previous sentence when I was completing an earlier draft of this book. I did not foresee the emotional anguish I felt when I forced myself to look at images of Malaysia Airlines Flight MH17, shot down over eastern Ukraine on Thursday 17 July. I have travelled by passenger jet a good deal in the last thirty years, and often with a child. And there were images of a child's teddy bear, a t-shirt, a Lonely Planet guidebook: I had not seen such an array of the intimate possessions of slaughtered innocent people since I visited the death camp museum of Auschwitz in 1997.

It is hard to retain any objectivity in the face of such pain and horror. It becomes difficult to ask the most basic questions. Yet an attempt at objectivity and the effort to ask questions must be made. Why was the airliner flying over eastern Ukraine, an area in which military transport planes had already been shot down? If MH17 was indeed shot down by a long range SA-11 'Buk' missile, then this weapon can reach aircraft at 72,000 feet. Passenger jets were ordered to fly at above 32,000 feet over eastern Ukraine — a typical altitude would be about 35,000 feet for an airliner. Simon Calder in *The Independent/i* of 19 July, quoting Jock Lowe, a former BA captain, was one of the few to consider this question. Airlines are among the most competitive enterprises that exist. Perhaps Malaysia Airlines — as well as the forces on the ground in Ukraine — should have provided answers.

This terrible incident cannot exclude consideration of the Ukrainian conflict as a whole, which is surrounded by a thicket of opinions, claims and counterclaims. Those who tend to defend Putin and Russia include — surprisingly — some people of left-wing outlook, some anti-European Conservatives, opponents of the European Union and a number of neo-Nazi groups, as well as those who try to face unpalatable realities honestly. From the first, Putin's Russia was acting upon the same ancient considerations: intense sensitivity about its status as a great power and what might be called a justified paranoia about strategic encirclement. Also, there is no evidence that the *Crimean* referendum was *only* an exercise carried out at the point of a Kalashnikov; certainly, Kalashnikovs abounded, but that does not necessarily mean that a majority of Crimeans did not want to be citizens of Russia.

In the coldest days of the Cold War, J.K. Paasikivi the President of Finland—the country that has fought the Russians longer and harder than any other—repeatedly referred to Russia's 'legitimate interests'. Those who point out that Russia still has such interests, nearly seventy years later, are not necessarily 'Putin's useful idiots' as Michael Mosbacher called them in the magazine *Standpoint* in the summer of 2014. The reality of Russia's position and Putin's attitude can be traced back to the conveniently forgotten fact that Britain has not even been able to conduct an intelligent foreign policy for years.

Despite Blair's desperate attempts to be a great international statesman, his actions and those of his circle look increasingly inept and silly, as does the posturing of David Cameron and William Hague and his successor Philip Hammond over Ukraine. How long will the outstanding British arms exports to Russia, embarrassingly still in place as Cameron called most loudly for a complete ban on arms sales to Moscow, be remembered? Or the 'coincidence' of the British government suddenly allowing a proper inquiry into the murder of the exiled Alexander Litvinenko after refusing it for seven years?

Blair's own lack of judgement led to occasions when he was castigated by Syria's President Assad and by Putin in public. The continuing problem of Russia has at least one specific cause. Individuals can change history when the objective conditions exist—or they can lamentably fail to do so. Lord George Robertson, Blair's Defence Secretary, later Secretary-General of NATO, was asked by Putin: 'When are you going to invite Russia to join NATO?' Robertson's answer was: 'Well, we don't invite countries, you apply.' Putin shrugged and said: 'Well, Russia isn't going to stand in the queue with a lot of countries that don't matter.'[3] After this snub, Putin—in his own eyes the leader of a Great World Power—never tried again.

David Cameron seemed to await hopefully the visit to the UK by Angela Merkel, the Chancellor of Germany, on 27 February 2014, during which she addressed both Houses of Parliament.

Presumably, he hoped for something to placate the right wing of his party and even something to help him out-manoeuvre UKIP. Such pressures had already led to the attention given to curtailing immigration. Chancellor Merkel offered some support on the idea of restrictions on how quickly new arrivals could claim benefits, but conceded nothing on the fundamental EU principle of free movement of citizens.

Cameron's attempt to prevent Jean-Claude Juncker becoming President of the European Commission was something that—surely—he knew could never succeed. This anti-European stunt was undertaken in order to please the Tory right wing, upstage UKIP, and provide justification for Britain's future withdrawal from Europe.

The government's own fiscal watchdog, The Office for Budget Responsibility, had already warned of the need for more migrant workers, not less, in order to keep public finances stable, because of the good effect of an influx of productive, working age migrants upon growth and on keeping down the national debt over the next fifty years. The argument is not difficult to grasp, and was spelt out in the OBR's annual long-term analysis in July 2013. Internally, Britain has an increasingly ageing and decreasingly productive population; migrant workers earn, spend and pay taxes, thus contributing to paying the public sector's debt and having 'a positive impact on the sustainability of public finances'.[4] And yet one of the few reasonably reliable guides to the British view of Europe is the *British Social Attitudes 30* report published by Natcen Social Research in 2013: 'Euroscepticism is firmly in the ascendancy, with a record 67% wanting either to leave or for Britain to remain but the EU to become less powerful.' The strength of that anti-Europeanism may well take Britain out of the European Union in the likely event that a referendum is held on membership.

Leaving aside the array of social, medical, commercial and economic advantages of European membership, we come to the bedrock fact that the European Union is the only one of the world's huge economic blocs to which we can belong on the basis of any kind of equality and partnership. Sentimental talk about the Commonwealth is nonsensical: the countries of the Commonwealth have long ago gone their own way. To remain part of Europe culturally and psychologically as well as politically and economically, or to leave it, will be the crucial question in the future of Britain in as far as that can in any way be foreseen. Very little in British society today gives cause for belief in a happy outcome. All too soon we are almost certain to see a President in Washington who is once again eager to make war on the enemies of the dwindling American empire. An isolated, impoverished Britain outside Europe will inevitably be dragged in America's wake as an even more despised underling state than it was made by Tony Blair during the War on Terror. The British also face the need to survive in a world in which global capitalism can never work properly and must repeatedly break down.

Following the treatment of the Chagossians by the Wilson government, the use of torture in Northern Ireland, the MI5 campaign against Scargill and the miners, and the Afghanistan and Iraq wars, the allegations of child abuse at Westminster should have come as no surprise: were they not inevitable? The bare facts are worth recording here because of the way in which such information is lost and distorted.

An MP called Geoffrey Dickens handed the Home Secretary Leon Brittan a dossier on the abuse of children by members of the establishment and senior politicians in 1983. On 3 July 2014 it was announced that the dossier had disappeared; and Brittan changed his story regarding it twice. The Home Office permanent secretary Mark Sedwill revealed that 114 files relating to child sex abuse had also disappeared. Simon Danczuk MP was warned by a senior Conservative MP *not* to name Leon Brittan. Perhaps most hideously of all, Tim Fortescue, a government whip when Heath was Prime Minister, had boasted in a BBC documentary in 1995 that whips could cover up 'scandals involving small boys' for MPs.

On Tuesday 8 July 2014, the British government appointed a retired senior judge, Baroness Elizabeth Butler-Sloss, aged eighty, as head of an inquiry into child abuse; this woman's *brother*, Sir Michael Havers, was Attorney General in the 1980s. Under pressure from MPs, the Baroness stepped down one week after her appointment. These events speak for themselves. If such things had happened in another country or in some earlier historical period, what conclusions would any sensible person draw? How warmly some members of the British establishment and some senior politicians must have welcomed the distracting events in Ukraine! How relieved they must have been to reach the long summer recess of Parliament!

Orwell said in 1941 that the 'real England' is 'still kept under by a generation of ghosts'. When we consider the permanent, unelected government from the Privy Council to the senior civil servants to the secret intelligence service inhabiting society like a tumour, we might want to change that to 'a generation of spooks'. We can only hope that some of the energies of the country that invented capitalism, socialism, industrialism and feminism and defied Hitler still remain.

[1] 'Hague urged to tell Spain ambassador to "pack his straw donkey and go" over Gibraltar row' (http://www.express.co.uk, last accessed on 02 February 2014).

[2] Matt Chorley, *Mailonline* Political Editor, 'Tory fury at "loopy Brazilian leftie" United Nations official who launched "political" attack on government welfare reforms', 11 September 2013 (http://www.dailymail.co.uk, last accessed 09 September 2013).

[3] This notorious exchange was most recently quoted in the BBC Radio 4 *Profile* documentary broadcast on 09 March 2014.

[4] Ben Chu, economics editor, '"Working-age" migrants needed to stem debt', *The Independent/i*, 18 July 2013.

Afterword

Liver Disease and Sociology

In May and June of 2013 I found myself, rather unexpectedly, in a hospital in South Wales, suffering from severe liver disease. When I arrived on an afternoon full of the still gloom of a low grey sky, the consultant admitted me on sight. He was a calm and indestructibly cheerful man, but he did tell me weightily that there is a thirty per cent mortality rate in cases in which the disease is as advanced as it obviously was in me.

'You mean that I have a seventy per cent chance of survival', I said brightly, and he nodded. Although I would make what they called 'a remarkable recovery' in the next weeks and months, I later discovered that both the consultant and my own GP thought that I would probably die at the time I went into hospital.

Solzhenitsyn begins his excellent short story *The Right Hand* —based on his experiences as a cancer patient in the 1950s—as follows: 'When I arrived in Tashkent that winter I was practically a corpse. I came there expecting to die.' But I did not feel like this at all. Despite my massively swollen belly, the dramatic amount of weight I had lost and my discoloured skin, I never believed that I would die, not even that there was a thirty per cent chance of my dying. I spent the first night in great pain and then in a remote state of blurred euphoria brought about by powerful injected painkillers. However, on my second full day in hospital, I dressed and went outside to walk around the car park on legs that were still tottering and unsteady. After that, I walked every day, in sunshine or in rain, ranging further and further around the hospital grounds and just outside them. I was convinced that the exercise was helping me to recover. I was deeply impressed by the care I was given by the nurses, mainly women, although there were a few male nurses, and by the doctors. I had never taken out medical insurance or paid into a private healthcare scheme in my life, and yet, apart from lacking a private room, I could not imagine being given any better care as a private patient. The humanity and warmth of the nurses were astonishing. My only cause for resentment was the way in which 'domestic' workers were treated—the people who cleaned the ward, the bathrooms and the toilets, as well as bringing and serving the meals. They seemed to be put upon by their own supervisors and treated as invisible—or with contempt—by most of the doctors and some of the nurses. I liked the cleaning and catering staff, and I hoped they liked me. One of them, a slim, tough woman with short dark hair, had left her work and showed me the way to the hospital shop and the main entrance on that first walk I took on my weak and uncertain legs. I channelled the frustration and tension that goes with any prolonged stay in hospital into standing up for them whenever I could and declaring loudly in front of doctors and nurses that the whole place would cease to function without their efforts.

Along with my daily exercise I kept my own written record of my condition as it changed day by day, as well as reading and writing. I was delighted when my wife asked me to write some extended notes for a student she was mentoring who was struggling with two essays on Marxism. One of the books beside my bed was *Marxism in the USA* by Paul Buhle, a gift from my daughter. One day, Tracy, an auxiliary nurse, picked it up and looked at it and began telling me that she had taken a degree in sociology, being thus overqualified for many jobs in the National Health Service. Fortunately, she liked the job she was doing. Things were not easy in my life at that time and the high dose of steroids I was taking often made my emotions seethe like a pan of pasta sauce with the heat turned up under it.

Tracy, with her stylish spiky hair, humour and easy gracefulness, was one of those women who improve and warm the atmosphere of any room they enter. Just before the dawn that followed a sleepless night, as I sat on my bed in tears, she sat beside me and talked to me and hugged me.

Some of the men who came to the ward stayed only a day or two and then went home. Others were clearly very ill or dying, and some were very elderly. One man in his thirties—at least twenty years younger than me—showed the same symptoms of liver disease as my own. Over about three weeks there was no improvement in this man's condition at all and he ceased getting out of bed. Almost certainly he died, at least, one morning he had disappeared from the room he occupied off the corridor that led into the ward—rooms that were given to patients who were more seriously ill and faced a long stay in hospital. The nurses had been talking about him in low, alarmed voices for days and repeatedly calling out the doctors to examine him.

One man had 'mental health issues', as the nurses put it when he was not near enough to hear them. After shouting at him on my first (pain-filled) night because of the noise he was making during a prolonged argument with a nurse, I got on well with him; he was highly intelligent, eccentric and starved of intelligent conversation. He was also either a troublemaker or someone who bitterly and relentlessly stood up for his rights, depending on how you looked at it.

About ten days before I went home, three men appeared on the ward within a day or two of each other and happened to be put in adjoining beds. They talked a great deal to each other, got on well and shared the same interests and views. These men wanted the television on more than anyone else had during my stay. The first programme they watched each day, with great amusement and enthusiasm, consisted of appearances by (apparently) normal and ordinary people who talked about their personal and sexual lives to an aggressive programme presenter, in front of a studio audience and thousands or millions of viewers across the country: wives and husbands confronting spouses who were having an affair, men with a gambling addiction who neglected their children, grown up children confronting the mother who had abandoned them in childhood, all of them degrading themselves publicly for the entertainment of others.

I kept my ear plugs in as I got on with reading and writing, but inevitably I overheard a good deal of the conversations between the newcomers on the ward. They were much concerned with foreigners coming to Britain, especially with the 'millions' of Romanians and Bulgarians who threatened to arrive and work here. A particularly savage attack was carried out by Muslims in London at this time—young men who were quickly arrested and charged. The three men across the ward from me seemed convinced that the perpetrators would 'get away with it' because of the colour of their skin and their religion. When the TV news announced that there were to be marches by the British National Party and the English Defence League, the three new patients reacted with delighted remarks that amounted almost to cheers.

I have always had trouble sleeping at night and I slept less than ever in hospital. When my eyes grew too tired to read I lay thinking about what I had overheard during the day. The lights of the ward—except for my own reading light behind the curtains around my bed—were dimmed almost to darkness and the oblivious silence was broken only by occasional snoring or other bodily noises. (When awake—at least when the female nurses were not within hearing distance—the three new men had the vilest manners of any of the patients I had encountered.)

Interestingly, as became clear from their conversations, these three men were not poor, disadvantaged, socially excluded or unemployed—they were prosperous working class. Also, all three of them were Welsh, not English. I wondered how typical they were. I wondered what their declared beliefs, the newspapers they read and the television programmes they liked might reveal about the state of Britain today. This book was born at about four in the morning in a hospital ward as the early summer dawn was turning the sky milk-coloured and mildly luminous.

George Orwell's brilliant, impressionistic and sometimes inaccurate book *The Lion and the Unicorn* was published in 1941, having been written during the worst of the London blitz. A later book by Orwell, *The English People,* was published in 1946; Orwell spoke of the later work with unjustified contempt. Actually, because the call for a left-wing, non-Marxist revolution in *The Lion and the Unicorn* was very much toned down in *The English People*, so that the reader is not distracted by the hoped for revolution that Orwell thought would grow out of the struggle against Hitler, but which did not occur, the later book is of greater value for us today.

In hospital I wondered if it would be possible to write a book about the mental climate of Britain in 2013 — a book more grounded in facts and research than the one Orwell was able to write in London in wartime, surrounded by the devastation caused by German bombs. Are some widely held attitudes signs and symptoms of a possible or probable future? I lay thinking of Derek Raymond's dystopian novel *A State of Denmark*, which I had read as a teenager in the 1970s — a book about a seedy dictatorship establishing itself in Britain; this was not the seedy dictatorship that some people in the 1970s and in 2013 believed and still believe already exists in the UK, but an out and out concentration camp and curfew dictatorship.

Tracy's mention of her degree in sociology reminded me of my copy of *The Sociological Imagination* by C. Wright Mills, a book I had lost. Mills was an American, of course, but a sociological imagination can be turned to any society. Meanwhile, I had about three hours in which to sleep. By seven in the morning the noise and bustle on the ward made further sleep impossible. There was clearly a great deal to be done. I had survived and now I must readjust, read, plan, think and then write. I had to get home and begin.

*

Recuperating during the hot weeks of June, I considered whether there were experiences in my past or journeys that I had made that I could draw upon in the effort to make some sense of the mental atmosphere of Britain today. Of course, to be born in a country and then to live in it for most of your life are the most relevant experiences of all. However, more specifically, I thought of my involvement with left-wing politics in the mid-1980s, when I had spent most of my days among people who thought of the present state of society as something to be replaced by a fundamentally different way of life. I had turned out on the picket lines during the Miners' Strike of 1984–85 as a gesture of solidarity, listening to those I met there and trying to understand the conflict as well as I could. And then, a little later on, I was dissatisfied with official explanations of the situation in Northern Ireland — almost everyone I knew and worked with was equally dissatisfied with such accounts — and so I went there to see for myself.

The BBC *Real Lives* programme about Northern Ireland, *At the Edge of the Union*, was banned in 1985. How evocative that title is! That is how it felt to be in Belfast at that time for someone who had known only mainland Britain — the sensation of standing at the faint, fading margins of a society, the place where another reality took hold. This was not just because of troops on the streets, the atmosphere of civil war and the frequency of violent death that was the consequence of the war. I followed the processions on 12 July, Orangeman's Day, through a city in which the physical divisions between communities and moral and psychological divisions coincided, standing out like the scars of wounds that had been crudely stitched up. Orangeman's Day at that time was an occasion and a spectacle unlike anything that could be seen in England, Wales and Scotland.

My parents tended to be right-wing in their outlook, at least during my childhood and adolescence. They attempted to bring me up to accept some of their convictions without question, as self-evident, such as 'Britain is the freest country in the world' (not that they had ever travelled beyond Britain). This belief may well be quite widely held even today. It may well have lingered in the back of my mind; associating with sincere people in left-wing circles tends to focus the mind upon the possibilities and limitations of capitalist parliamentary democracy at home, which is a perspective that ignores how much capitalist countries vary. I did not re-examine this belief properly until my partner and I spent the summer of 1988 in Finland. When we returned people asked me what Finland had been like. I said that I found Finland strange at first because I was suddenly in a free country, which naturally brought condescending smiles and murmurs about how easy it is to idealize things.

However, we had gone to Finland with very little money, which has usually been the case wherever I have travelled, from Arctic Norway to North Africa and from Ireland to Turkey. I recall landing late at night and taking the airport bus into the centre of Helsinki, getting off with our rucksacks in the darkness of the brief northern night. We intended to camp during our time in Finland, and preferably to save money by putting our tent anywhere we could, rather than on official campsites. Whereas I was weary, my partner—who was pregnant—was exhausted.

We put the tent on the nearest stretch of grass under some trees and awoke next morning to find that we were in the grounds of Finlandia Hall, international conference centre and meeting place of the leaders of East and West. We were also visible from one of the main streets in Helsinki, but instead of flashing lights and men with machine guns, no one took any notice of us. For the next three nights we camped on Seurasaari, an open air museum where historic buildings had been brought from all over Finland and reconstructed. No officious park wardens told us to move on and no one vandalized our tent.

Helsinki, I thought, had something missing: it turned out to be poverty. There were richer areas and poorer areas, but no slums and nothing remotely like the inner city areas of London, Manchester or Birmingham, or the problem council estates attached to most British towns and cities.

In Hameenlinna, northwest of Helsinki, when we asked for directions from a middle-aged woman, she cycled after us with a photocopied map of the town from the library. When we were exhausted and set down at an inconvenient spot while hitch-hiking in eastern Finland, we knocked at the door of a house and asked if we could buy a coffee somewhere nearby. The family simply invited us to camp in their garden and brought us coffee and invited us to breakfast next morning. And when we caught the wrong connection in central Finland and found ourselves on a train taking us in entirely the wrong direction, the ticket inspector reacted with sympathy and showed us the right platform at the next station. Dozens of similar incidents built up over the weeks to reinforce the sense of being in a country in which people were not afraid of each other or of foreigners, in which a culture of freedom and an assumption of equality formed a constant background.

The Finns can hardly be said to have had it easy. They have not spent the last two centuries in the privileged situation of Switzerland. Until the 1960s Finland was a much poorer country than Britain, as well as being the only neighbour of the Soviet Union to maintain a Western style democracy. Unlike British government ministers (particularly in the 1980s) Finnish government ministers did not make speeches justifying nuclear missiles as an essential means of preserving 'liberty', getting on instead with the business of freedom and survival as a frontline state in the Cold War of the fifties and sixties and in the second Cold War of the eighties.

In recent years, after the collapse of the Soviet Union and then Finnish membership of the European Union, extreme right wing groups have arisen in Finland, and more recently something equivalent to UKIP, the UK Independence Party. The Conservatives in Britain worry about UKIP winning over their traditional supporters and tend to be cautious accordingly. Too much support for gay rights runs the risk of offending the faithful. In Scandinavia traditional reactionary sensibilities about marriage, the family and gender are not there to be offended, and so anti-European groups cannot boost their support in this roundabout way. When I revisited Finland I found the culture of freedom a little battered and scratched but still very much there. The problem of public drunkenness was also much the same. One of the innumerable jokes the Finns make up about themselves goes like this: you can always tell the Somalis in Helsinki from the native Finns—the Somalis dress in neat suits and are sober.

I read and reread Orwell's *The Lion and the Unicorn* and *The English People* ('that silly little *English People* book' as Orwell called it, with almost pathological modesty, in a letter to Julian Symons in 1947) in the weeks after I returned home from hospital. Orwell had served with the Imperial Police in Burma for five years, lived in Paris for two years and lived and fought in Spain during the Spanish Civil War. He is incisive and perceptive about Britain because he can draw upon his experiences of other countries and very different conditions. This is necessarily so. You cannot know the standard of football in your own country unless your country plays football with the national teams of other countries. It is impossible to judge how well medicine is practised in one country without some information about the care of the sick in other countries. To say that the law is (even) more oppressive in Italy than in Britain, that the crime rate is high and petty theft is common in Naples and Rome, that the piles of rubbish beside roads and the pollution show that the Italians have a disregard for the environment that would not be tolerated in Britain is not to idealize the British or ignore Italy's virtues.

Sadly, the British are too often incapable of seeing Britain as a piece in the mosaic of European societies, despite decades of cheap travel. They have forgotten the line from Kipling, one of their most enthusiastic gutter patriots: 'What do they know of England who only England know?' For example, several of our nearest neighbours are republics—Finland, Iceland and Ireland (I deliberately omit France). The impressive beginnings of parliamentary democracy in northern Europe were made in Iceland, not in Britain as is fondly believed. As for Ireland, the first woman to become the President of the Republic, Mary

Robinson, transformed the office to which she was elected and transformed the image of Ireland abroad and the way in which the Irish perceived themselves. After her seven-year term of office, she declined to seek a second term, becoming UN High Commissioner for Human Rights. And yet some educated people in Britain still justify the continued existence of the monarchy by saying: 'Of course, whatever the faults of a constitutional monarchy, republics are much worse.' Is there a member of the British Royal Family whose achievements equal those of Mary Robinson? The half-conscious belief that what the British do not do cannot be done ripples far too often under the surface of life in Britain.

I lived in Spain for two years between 1991 and 1993, mainly in Andalucia, the poorest and largest region of Spain in the days of Franco and in the 1990s. Yet economic deprivation did not breed crime and violence in the rural area in which we lived; people in most English and Welsh villages I had been in—particularly young people—were far more aggressive. Even the large southern cities of Malaga and Algeciras were far less threatening than most British (or Italian) cities. In the rural villages there was no vandalism, telephone boxes and public seats were not broken or defaced, and children were welcome in every bar, although alcohol was not sold to those under sixteen.

The sullen aggression that pervades drinking places in Britain was unknown. This was an area of great unemployment, but the social security laws seemed to ease the situation. Those receiving benefit were required to do sixty days community service each year. Such a law hovered in the background as an oppressive spectre in Britain, but its implementation in Andalucia was quite different. The local elected mayor had some real power in these mountain villages (which is not to say that he was always popular or that he was never resented). And it was the mayor who authorized the payment of benefits *and* provided most of the informal cash-in-hand jobs, although technically the law denied benefits to those doing paid work. Those doing community service were allowed to leave it whenever any cash-in-hand work came their way; there were no authoritarian Job Clubs or punitive Youth Training Schemes. The British, German and Danish 'exiles', some of whom had lived in the area for many years, were accepted as part of the community by the Andalucians, even—or rather especially—those who were extremely poor.

I wrote an article on the way of life of the area for the magazine *Social Care Education*, which was published in the winter 1991/92 edition, and before I sent it off I read it to some of the English-speaking exiles who had lived in the area for some years; they had, after all, provided me with much of my information.

There was no church and no priest in the village in which we lived, although there was a church hall. Even before the Spanish Civil War, and especially during the war, large numbers of the Spanish poor had come to the realization that the Roman Catholic Church in Spain was simply part of the machinery of oppression—something which the Franco dictatorship confirmed yet again. On the other hand, no one objected to a priest coming to the church hall to conduct Catholic weddings, which were becoming popular with some young people. The village had a solitary and unarmed officer of the *Policia Local*. The community was indeed self-regulating and self-policing, which was an expression of the anarchist and socialist tradition of the mountain villages. The tradition was receding somewhat under the pressure of social change in the 1990s, and yet it was still alive. But anarchism and socialism of that kind can never work! So people fondly believe—especially in Britain... Until or unless they happen to see it working.

As I reflected on British social attitudes and how they might influence the future, my pessimism increased as my health steadily improved. I also felt that Britain's future is inseparable from the state of the world, which has given very little cause for optimism since 11 September 2001.

The veteran Marxist Terry Eagleton is blunt in his appraisal of the state of the world:

> For the first time in history, our prevailing form of life has the power not simply to breed racism and spread cultural cretinism,

drive us into war or herd us into labour camps, but to wipe us from the planet... What used to be apocalyptic fantasy is today no more than sober realism. The traditional leftist slogan 'Socialism or barbarism' was never more grimly apposite, never less of a mere rhetorical flourish.[1]

This may well be so. However, we must return to Tolstoy's famous opening line in *Anna Karenina*. 'All happy families resemble one another, but each unhappy family is unhappy in its own way.' Thus, all humane societies may resemble one another, but each barbaric society is barbaric in its own way. If Britain faces a grim future, that future will grow out of the distinctive attitudes and features of British society and out of the intersection of those attitudes and features with the state of the world, which will affect Britain and every other country. The mental climate of some countries may make them more able to resist disaster and the mental climate of other societies may make them slide into disaster more easily. The evidence needed for a clear understanding of the consequences of our attitudes is surely all around us in the words we hear and read every day.

[1] Terry Eagleton, *Why Marx Was Right*, New Haven & London, 2011.

Index

Abbott, Pamela 38, 62
Aberfan disaster (1966) 68
abortion (legalisation) 15
Acheson, Sir Donald 69, 77
Adams, Gerry 41–2
Adebowale, Lord 61
Afghanistan 48, 57–9, 64, 79, 135
Africa 9, 10, 11, 48, 102–3, 110, 114, 115
Aftermath, The (Churchill) 33
Age of Extremes (Hobsbawm) 11, 61
Akhmatova, Anna 97
Albania 86
Alfie 14
Ali, Muhammad 27
Alibhai-Brown, Yasmin 58–9, 63
All Quiet on the Western Front (Remarque) 83
Allardice, Lisa 115
Allen, Kevin 74
America (see also USA) 2, 5, 16, 17, 20, 27, 28, 42, 45, 47, 53, 55–6, 57, 59, 87, 91, 118, 120, 122, 129, 135

American Tragedy, An (Dreiser) 95
Amery, Leo 46
Amis, Kingsley 106–7
Amnesty International 22, 62
Amritsar massacre 10
Anna Karenina (Tolstoy) 1, 148
anti-Semitism 86
anti-terrorist legislation 10, 95
Areopagitica (Milton) 96
Argentina/Argentines 32, 38–9
Arkins, Brian 71
Arthur, Chris 83
Ashdown, Lord 57
Asia 10
Assad, President (Syria) 133
At the Edge of the Union (BBC) 142
Atos Healthcare 61, 130
Attlee, Clement 3, 29
Auel, Jean M. 110
Aung San Suu Kyi 90
Auschwitz 18, 132
Australia 37, 67, 111
Austria 7, 121

Avengers, The 14
Axelsson, Majgull 119
Ayatollah Khomeini 87

BAE Systems 54
Baker, Joanne 81
Bakewell, Joan 3, 14
Bank of England 50
Barstow, Stan 108
Bashevis Singer, Isaac 120
Bavaria 20
BBC 60, 131, 142
Beatles, The 13
Beckham, David 91–2
'bedroom tax' 61, 129–31
Belfast 21, 142
Belloc, Hilaire 92
Bellow, Saul 120
Belmarsh prison 10
Belmont psychiatric unit 18
Benn, Tony 19, 22, 43, 78, 89–90, 122
Berlin 28
Bevan, Aneurin 33, 34, 72–3, 83–4
Bevan, W. 72
Beyond the Fringe 13
'Black Wednesday' (1992) 48
Blair, Cherie 53, 56
Blair, Tony 8, 15, 22, 34, 39, 44, 49, 50, 52–7, 58, 59–60, 62, 63, 91–2, 99, 130, 133, 135
Blix, Hans 55, 130
Bolshevik Revolution (1917) 3, 86, 104
Book of Common Prayer 81
Boston College 42

Boy in the Bubble, The (Paul Simon) 3
Boyle, Danny 74
Bradbury, Malcolm 118
Bradford, Sarah 83, 85
Braine, John 107–8, 114, 120
Brecht, Bertolt 104
Brezhnev, Leonid/ 'Brezhnev Doctrine' 19, 53
Brighton bombing (1984) 46
British Empire 11
British Establishment 26, 122
British Indian Ocean Territory 15, 17
British literature 9, 94–126
British National Party (BNP) 140
British Social Attitudes 134
Brittan, Leon 135
Bronowski, Jacob 84–5, 93, 105
Brooke, Rupert 101
Brooks, Geraldine 95
Brown, Gordon 50, 52, 59–60, 64, 92
Buhle, Paul 138
Bulgarians 140
Burgess, Anthony 100, 109, 117–8
Burma 145
Burton, Richard 9
Bush, George W. 8, 47, 53, 55, 56, 58, 59, 64, 130
Butler-Sloss, Elizabeth (Baroness) 135–6

Caetano, Marcello 28
Caine, Michael 13

Calder, Simon 132
Callaghan, James 25, 31, 33
'Camelot' style government 13
Cameron, David 44, 52, 60, 64, 82–3, 91, 105, 133
Campaign for Nuclear Disarmament (CND) 23, 44, 103
Camus, Albert 113
Canada 5
Cancer Ward (Solzhenitsyn) 95, 125
capital punishment 14–5
capitalism 17, 19, 36, 48, 52, 70, 97, 122, 135, 136, 143
Cardiff 71
Cardiff Law School 10
Castle, Barbara 30
Casual Vacancy, The (J.K. Rowling) 78, 120–6
Cathy Come Home 14
CCTV surveillance 95
Central Office of Information 89
Centre of the Bed, The (Joan Bakewell) 3, 14
Ceuta 127
Chagos Archipelago 15, 16, 17, 87
Chagossians 16, 19, 20, 48, 87, 89, 135
Chalfont, Lord 16
Chamberlain, Neville 7, 46, 53
Champion, George 16–7

Charles, Prince of Wales 80–2, 88–9, 92
Chesterton, G.K. 122
child abuse allegations (Westminster) 135–6
China 85
Chomsky, Noam 19
Chorley, Matt 129, 136
Christianity 2, 56
Christie, Julie 13
Church of England 83, 88
Churchill, Caryl 36, 98
Churchill, Winston 3–4, 6, 29, 33–4, 55, 80
class system (British) 3
Clegg, Nick 64
climate change 95
Clinton, Bill 59
Clockwork Orange, A (Burgess/Kubrick) 100, 117
Coalition government (2010–15) 37, 51, 60, 76, 129
Cold War 4, 6, 7, 24, 25, 133, 144
Collins, Michael 71
Coming Up for Air (Orwell) 95–6
Commonwealth (British) 135
Communist Manifesto, The (Marx and Engels) 36, 72
Communist Party (British) 4, 104, 114
Communist Party (Czechoslovak) 6, 24
Communist Party (Finnish) 24

Communist Party (French) 24
Communist Party (Italian) 24
Congress (US) 16
Conlon, Gerry 15
Conrad, Joseph 102, 106, 115
consensus politics 24, 25
Conservative Party/governments 3, 4, 11, 16, 20, 22, 23, 25, 26, 28, 30–1, 43, 44, 45, 47, 48, 51, 66, 72, 77, 80, 100, 117, 129, 132, 144
Contemporary Review 83
Cook, Robin 15, 54
corporal punishment 18
Corridors of Power (Snow) 105
Corrigan, Maire 21
Creasy, Stella (MP) 49
Crick, Bernard 98
Crimea 132–3
Crisis Decades 25, 29, 58
Cuba 38, 81
Curtis, Mark 16
Czech Republic 92
Czechoslovakia 6, 7, 19–20, 24, 28, 53, 95

Daily Express 127
Daily Mail 1, 7, 17, 32, 78, 85, 121
Daily Mirror 40
Daily Telegraph 31
Danczuk, Simon (MP) 135
Daniel Martin (Fowles) 117, 126
Darling 14
Das Kapital (Marx) 94
Dawson, S.W. 112, 113, 126

Day of the Women, The (Kettle) 99–100
death penalty (abolition) 14–5
Demon-Haunted World, The (Sagan) 76
Denmark 24, 92
Department for Work and Pensions 105, 131
Derry 21
De Valera, Eamon 71
Diana, Princess of Wales 49
Dickens, Charles 14, 94, 105, 106, 122
Dickens, Geoffrey (MP) 135
Diego Garcia 15, 16, 17
Doctor Zhivago (Pasternak) 26
Dodsworth, Martin 119–20
Donaldson, Mr Justice (Lord) 15
Dostoyevsky, Fyodor 115, 123, 125
Douglas-Home, Alec 13
Drabble, Margaret 114
Drakeford, Mark 66
Dreiser, Theodore 95, 123
Duffy, Carol Ann 92, 97
Dunkirk 18
Dunmore, Helen 95

Eagleton, Terry 43, 147–8
Eastern Europe 6, 19, 53, 118
Eden, Anthony 4, 5, 7, 8, 48
Edward VIII 82
Egypt 4, 5, 7, 8, 9, 11, 25, 89
Eliot, George (Mary Ann Evans) 14, 94, 104, 105, 106, 114

Elizabeth II 15, 80, 82, 83, 84, 85, 86, 87, 89, 91–2
Emadi, Hafizullah 83
Emmerdale Farm 73
Employment and Support Allowance (ESA) 51
Enemy Within, The (Seumas Milne) 41, 62
Engels, Frederick 72
English Defence League (EDL) 140
English People, The (Orwell) 76, 96, 141, 145
Ethiopia 86
European Economic Area (EEA) 70
European Economic Community (EEC) 24, 28, 71
European Exchange Rate Mechanism 48
European Security Conference (Helsinki, 1975) 26
European Union 24, 28, 39, 65, 70–1, 128, 132, 134–5, 144
Evans, Dick 54
Existentialism 125

Falklands Crisis/War 4, 16, 35, 38–9, 48, 90
Fascism 86, 128
Faulks, Sebastian 95
FBI 27
Female Eunuch, The (Greer) 30, 97
feminism/feminists 30, 48–9, 99–100, 115, 116, 136
financial crisis (2008) 48, 60

Financial Times 50
Finland 6, 24, 26, 69–70, 91, 95, 121, 133, 143–5
finlandization 24
Finney, Albert 13
First World War 33
Fonda, Jane 19, 27, 55–6, 122
food banks 61, 95
Foot, Michael 34, 43, 90
Fortescue, Tim 135
Fowles, John 109, 116–7, 126
France 2, 5, 6, 7, 8, 11, 91, 113, 116, 121, 145
Franco, General Francisco 28, 146, 147
Fraud Squad 41
Frost, David 14

Gaddafi, Colonel (Libya) 40–1
Galileo 81
Germany 6, 28, 86, 121, 133–4
Germany (East/German Democratic Republic) 53
Gibraltar 23, 28, 127–8
Gillan, Cheryl 65
globalization 70, 95
'God Save the Queen' 80
Golden Age of capitalism 11, 12, 19, 22, 25, 37, 50
Golden Notebook, The (Lessing) 114–5, 122
Golding, William 109–12, 116, 117, 118
Gorbachev, Mikhail 53
Gordimer, Nadine 120
grammar schools 18
Great Plague 95

Greatbatch, Sir Bruce 15
Greece 116
Green Party 67
Greene, Graham 102–3, 106, 112, 114, 116, 123
Greenwood, Anthony 17, 86–7
Greer, Germaine 19, 30, 81, 97
Grove, Eric 57
Guardian, The 4, 40, 41, 115
Guildford Four 15
Gulag Archipelago, The (Solzhenitsyn) 42
Gwilym, Dafydd ap 73

Hague, William 127, 133, 136
Hain, Peter 64–5
Hammond, Philip 133
Hanley, Michael 23
Hari, Johann 42, 59, 62, 64, 77
Harry Potter (J.K. Rowling) 49, 101, 120
Havers, Sir Michael 136
Haw, Brian 17
Hawking, Stephen 92
Healey, Denis 25, 43
Heart of Darkness (Conrad) 102, 106
Heath, Edward 22, 23–6, 41, 45, 54, 105, 135
Helsinki 26, 143, 144, 145
Hemingway, Ernest 94, 102, 118
Heptonstall, Geoffrey 83
High Court 87, 90
Hitchens, Christopher 59, 63, 81, 82, 92

Hitler, Adolf 5, 6, 7, 28, 33, 34, 35, 40, 48, 53, 86, 88, 136, 141
Hobbit, The (Tolkien) 100
Hobsbawm, Eric 1, 4, 11, 25, 31–2, 38, 44, 50, 61, 62, 98
Hola prison camp (Kenya) 9–10
Homer 96
homo sapiens 110
homosexuality (legalisation) 15
Housing Benefit 51
Howe, Geoffrey 45–6
Huggins, Robert 69
Hungary/Hungarian National Rising 1, 4, 5–7, 20, 53
Hussein, Saddam (Iraq) 2, 5, 56, 130

Ibsen, Henrik 98
Iceland/Icelandic language 75, 91, 145
immigrants/immigration 52, 134, 140
In Place of Fear (Bevan) 83–4
'income poverty' 36
Independent/i, The 23, 40, 60, 61, 64, 65, 131, 132
India 10
Indonesia 54
Industrial Relations Act 24
Inland Revenue 41
Institute for Fiscal Studies 60
interest rates 50
Interesting Times (Hobsbawm) 50, 61, 62

International Criminal Court 16
IRA (Irish Republican Army — Provisional) 23, 42, 46, 115
Iraq/Iraq War 8, 15, 17, 47, 48, 49, 53, 55–7, 58–9, 89, 130, 135
Ireland/Irish Republic 24, 28, 48, 71, 91, 143, 145–6
'Iron Curtain Speech' (Churchill) 4
ISIS (Islamic State of Iraq and the Levant) 56
Islam 88
Islamist terrorism 56–9, 140
Israel/Israelis 5, 25, 28
Italy 86, 99, 145, 146

'Jack the Giant-Killer' 48
Jackson, Stewart 130
Jakobson, Max 54, 61
'James Bond' 14
James, Emma Anne 35, 74, 77
Jelinek, Elfriede 121, 122
Jesus 2, 88
jihadist terrorism 56–9, 140
Jimmy Porter (*Look Back in Anger*) 9, 11, 106, 107
Jobseekers' Allowance 51
Johnson, Boris 57
Johnson, Lyndon 16
Jones, Ieuan Wyn 65, 66
Joseph Rowntree Foundation 60
Journal of Law and Society 10
Joyce, Graham 119
Joyce, James 104, 118
Juan Carlos, King (Spain) 28

July 7 bombings (London, 2005) 57, 58
Juncker, Jean-Claude 134

Kampfner, John 55, 63
Keeler, Christine 12–3
Kekkonen, Urho (President of Finland) 24
Kennedy, John F. 13, 54
Kenya 9–10
Kettle, Pamela 99–100
KGB (Soviet Intelligence) 23
Khomeini, Ayatollah 87
Khrushchev, Nikita 20, 25, 26
Kikuyu tribe (Kenya) 9–10
Kinnock, Neil 42–5, 49, 50
Kipling, Rudyard 10, 105, 145
Koran, The 56
Korbut, Olga 28
Krupskaya, Nadezhda (Lenin's wife) 19
Kubrick, Stanley 117
Kumar, Krishan 13–4
Kurten, Bjorn 110

Labour Party/governments 1, 3, 13, 14–5, 16, 17, 22, 25, 26, 31–2, 37, 42–4, 48, 49–50, 52, 54, 55, 66, 72, 73, 77, 83–4, 87, 90, 99, 105
Lady Chatterley's Lover (Lawrence) 12, 14
Latin America 23, 120
Lawrence, D.H. 12, 73, 95
Le Carre, John 14
Leicester 10, 59
Lenin, V.I. 19, 33–4, 84, 86

Lessing, Doris 98, 104, 114–5, 116, 119, 120, 122
Lewis, Saunders 72–3
Liberal Democrats 44, 65, 66, 77, 129
Liberal Party 13, 24, 44
Liddle, Roger 50, 62
Life of Brian (Monty Python) 88
Lightman, Gavin (QC) 41
Lion and the Unicorn, The (Orwell) 3, 10, 54, 96, 141, 145
Literature and Western Man (Priestley) 94, 102
literature, British 9, 94–126
Litvinenko, Alexander 133
London bombings (7 July 2005) 57, 58
London, Jack 123
Look Back in Anger (Osborne) 9, 98, 106
Lord of the Rings, The (Tolkien) 100–1, 109
Lowe, Captain Jock 132
Lowell, Robert 73
Lucky Jim (Amis) 106–7

Macmillan, Harold 8, 11, 12–3, 54, 105
Magus, The (Fowles) 116
Mailonline 129
Major, John 47–8, 52, 59
Malamud, Bernard 120
Malaysia Airlines Flight MH17 132
Mandela, Nelson 90
Mandelson, Peter 50, 62
Mao Zedong 85

Marx, Karl 36, 56, 94, 122, 148
Marxism 2, 7, 34, 36, 56, 72, 138
Marxism in the USA (Buhle) 138
Marxists 18, 34, 71–2, 147
Mau Mau (Kenya) 9–10
Mauritius 16, 17, 87
Maw, James 18, 62
McConville, Jean 42
McWilliam, Candia 112–3
Mein Kampf (Hitler) 34
Melilla 127
Mengele, Dr Joseph 18
mental health 18, 61, 115, 139
Merkel, Angela 121, 133–4
Meyer, Sir Christopher 57
MI5 23, 40–2, 135, 136
Middle East 28
'middle England' 14, 18, 26, 121
Middlemarch (George Eliot; Mary Ann Evans) 104
Miliband, Ed 1
Miliband, Ralph 78
Militant Tendency (Labour Party) 43
Mills, C. Wright 141
Milne, Seumas 40–1, 62
Milton, John 96–7
miners 8, 23, 24, 32, 40–1, 44–5, 67–8, 84, 103, 135
Miners' Strike (1984–85) 34, 40–1, 42–3, 45, 142
Moir, Jan 121
monarchy (British) 78–93, 146

Montreal 26
Morocco 127
Mosbacher, Michael 133
Moscow 53, 133
Moylan, John 60
Munich 26, 28
Munson, James 83–7, 90–2
Murdoch, Iris 109, 112–4, 116, 117
Muslims 121, 129, 140
Mussolini, Benito 86
My Life So Far (Jane Fonda, 2005) 55–6

Nabokov, Vladimir 120
Naipaul, V.S. 120
Nasser, President (Egypt) 5
Natcen Social Research 134
National Archives, Kew 17
National Health Service (NHS) 3, 18, 35, 137–8
National Union of Mineworkers (NUM) 40–1, 42–3, 44–5
nationalization 3
Native Americans 110
NATO 133
Nazis/Nazism 6, 22, 40, 80, 86, 88, 116, 118, 128
Neanderthal humans 110
neo-Nazi groups 52, 59, 76, 128–9, 132
'New Labour' 37, 48, 50, 53
New Statesman 40, 127–8
New York 38
Nineteen Eighty-Four (Orwell) 2, 4, 98–9, 123
Nixon, Richard 16, 27, 53

Nobel Peace Prize 21
Nobel Prize for Literature 115, 121
North Africa 143
Northern Ireland 20–2, 41–2, 59, 135, 142
Norway 70, 92, 143

Oak and the Calf, The (Solzhenitsyn) 118
Obama, Barack 53–4
Observer, The 40, 97
Office for Budget Responsibility (OBR) 134
Oil Crisis (1973–74) 25
Olympic Games 26, 28
Orangemen (Northern Ireland) 142
Orbis 95
Orwell, George 2, 3, 4, 7, 10–1, 34, 45, 47–8, 54, 70, 76, 95–6, 98–9, 101, 102–3, 106, 123, 128, 136, 141, 145
Osborne, John 9, 11, 98, 106, 107
Owen, Lord David 18

Paasikivi, J.K. (President of Finland) 133
Paine, Thomas 91
Paisley, Ian (Jr.) 127–8
Palestine/Palestinians 28, 83
Palmer, Alan 20, 62
Paris 27, 145
Pasternak, Boris 26, 120
Peirce, Gareth 10
Pentagon, The 16
Peru 39
Phelps, Gilbert 106

Pilger, John 15, 17, 53, 62, 89, 93, 98
Plaid Cymru (Welsh Nationalists) 65–7, 75, 76, 77
Planet: The Welsh Internationalist 73, 77
Poland 53
Polaris nuclear submarine 16
Police Service of Northern Ireland (PSNI) 42
Politics and the English Language (Orwell) 7
'poll tax' 47, 130
Portugal 27–8
post-liberal social control 22, 41
poverty 36–8, 60–1
Poverty and Social Exclusion Project (2014) 60
Powell, Anthony 104, 106
Powell, Enoch 9–10
Prague 6, 20
Pravda 86
Prescott, Lord 57
Priestley, J.B. 94, 102
Prince Charles 80–2, 88–9, 92
Private Eye 13
Privy Council 15, 17, 89–90, 136
Profumo, John 12–3
Proust, Marcel 104–5, 106
psychiatric patients 18, 61
psychiatrists/psychiatry 18, 81, 119
Putin, Vladimir 121, 132–3

Quant, Mary 13

Queen Elizabeth II 15, 80, 82, 83, 84, 85, 86, 87, 89, 91–2

Raffles and Miss Blandish (Orwell) 47–8
Raymond, Derek 99, 100, 141
Reagan, Ronald 7
recession (post 2008) 60
Reece, Gordon 33
religion/religious belief 56, 87–8, 91, 110, 111–2, 122
Resurrection (Tolstoy) 95
Rhodesia 114, 119
Richard III (Shakespeare) 32
Right Hand, The (Solzhenitsyn) 137
Road to Wigan Pier, The (Orwell) 96, 128
Roberts, Geoffrey 4, 61
Robertson, Lord George 133
Robinson, Mary (President of Ireland) 28, 48, 71, 145–6
Rogers, Pat 120
Rolling Stones, The 13
Rolnik, Raquel 129–30
Roman Catholicism 72, 101–3, 112, 147
Romanians 140
Roosevelt, Franklin D. 6
Rothschild, Victor 41
Rowling, J.K. 19, 49, 78, 88, 92, 101, 120–6
Royal Family (British) 78–93, 146
Runciman, David 8, 61
Rushdie, Salman 87
Russell, Bertrand 27

Russia (see also Soviet Union) 6, 7, 19, 95, 97, 114, 120, 121, 126, 132–3
Russian Revolution 1917 3, 86, 104

Saddam Hussein (Iraq) 2, 5, 56, 130
Sagan, Carl 76
St Francis of Assisi 33
Salazar, Antonio 28
Salmond, Alex 66
Sargant, William 18, 19
Sartre, Jean-Paul 113
SAS 22, 23
Satanic Verses, The (Rushdie) 87
Scargill, Arthur 40–1, 78, 88, 135
Scotland 64, 65, 66–7, 70, 73–4, 75, 142
Scottish National Party (SNP) 65, 66–7, 70
Scrooge (*A Christmas Carol*) and capitalism 52
Second World War 3, 9, 25, 61, 80, 95, 97, 102, 119, 131, 141
Sedwill, Mark 135
September 11th 2001 22, 41, 57–8, 90, 147
sex/sexual attitudes 12–3, 14, 109, 144
Seychelles 15
Seymour-Smith, Martin 104, 105, 118
Shakespeare, William 32, 102, 106, 107

Shapps, Grant 129
Shaw, George Bernard 98
Shelley, Percy Bysshe 97
Short, Clare 49, 55, 57
Shrimpton, Jean 13
Sillitoe, Alan 108
Simon, Paul 3
Sinn Fein 41–2
Sinyavsky, Andrei 120
Sixties, The (1960s) 11–22, 27, 105, 108
Slovakia 19, 20
Smith, John 49
Snow, C.P. 104–5, 120
Snowden, Edward 59
Social Care Education 147
Social Democratic Party/Social Democrats (UK) 43–4, 49, 118
Socialist Workers' Party (UK) 23
Solzhenitsyn, Alexander 20, 26, 42, 73, 81, 83, 90, 95, 118, 120, 121, 122, 125, 126, 137
Somalis 145
Somerset floods (2014) 82
South Georgia (Falkland Islands) 38
Soviet Union (see also USSR) 3, 5, 6, 7, 20, 23, 24, 25, 26, 27, 40, 41, 42, 53, 81, 97, 103, 118, 120, 121, 126, 144
Spain 11, 28, 47, 79, 127–8, 145, 146–7
Spark, Muriel 112
Spitz, Mark 28
Spycatcher (Wright) 23, 41

Stalin, Josef 1, 4, 6, 8, 17, 20, 25, 26, 33, 38, 85–6, 104
Stalinism 1, 2, 25
Stamp, Terence 13
Standpoint (magazine) 133
State of Denmark, A (Raymond) 99, 141
Stephens, Michael 57
Stewart, Michael 17
Stone, Oliver 53
Storey, David 108–9
student radicalism 18–9
Suez Crisis 4–5, 7–9, 11, 39, 48, 55
Sun, The 31, 40, 73, 79
Swansea 44, 47, 72, 74, 80, 112
Sweden 70, 92, 94–5, 119, 121
Swift, Jonathan 106
Switzerland 7, 70, 71, 144
Symons, Julian 145
Syria 25, 133

Thatcher, Margaret 4, 7, 8, 20, 22, 25, 29–41, 42–3, 45–8, 50, 52, 53, 54, 55, 56, 62, 80, 90, 99–100, 103, 114, 129, 130, 131
'Third World' 23
Thomas, Dylan 73
Thomas, Philip A. 10, 61
Thomas, R.S. 73
Thompson, Piers 69
Tolkien, J.R.R. 100–1, 109, 112
Tolstoy, Leo 1, 19, 78, 91, 95, 105, 107, 148

Tory Party/Tories (see also Conservative Party/governments) 72, 134
trade unions 17–8, 24, 26, 31–2, 72, 88
Trainspotting 73–4
Tripp, John 73
Trotsky, Leon 84
Trotskyism 43, 44
Truman, Harry S. 4, 6, 7
Turgenev, Ivan 19
Turkey 143
Twiggy 13
Twin Town 73–5
'two cultures' (C.P. Snow) — science and literature 105

UK Competitiveness Index (UKCI) 69–70
Ukraine 20, 131–3
Ulster Peace Movement 21
Ulyanov, Alexander (Lenin's brother) 19
Ulysses (Joyce) 104
unemployment 11, 50–1, 67, 68–9, 82, 86, 146–7
United Kingdom Independence Party (UKIP) 128–9, 134, 144
United Nations (UN) 5, 16, 36–7, 47, 48, 55, 81, 129–30
Up the Junction 14
Upward, Edward 103–4
USA/United States of America (see also America) 39, 55, 91, 95, 99
USSR (see also Soviet Union) 25, 103

Vidal, Gore 19, 59
Vietnam 27, 56
Viggers, Peter (MP) 49
Viren, Lasse 26, 28
voting age 14

Wade, Helen 127-8
Wain, John 107
Wales 64-77, 82, 137, 142, 146
Wallace, Claire 38, 62
Walsh, Jill Paton 95
War and Peace (Tolstoy) 104
'War on Terror' 8, 22, 41, 53, 58, 135
Warsaw Pact 7
Washington 53, 135
Watergate scandal 27
Waters, Sarah 95
Weapons of Mass Destruction (WMD) 8, 47, 55, 130
Welsh Assembly 65-70
Welsh language 75-6
Welsh nationalism 64-77
Western Europe 26-7, 67
When Poetry keeps Faith and Fiction Does Not (Anthony James) 95
Whitehouse, Mary 14, 107
Who, The 13

Why Marx Was Right (Eagleton) 43, 147-8
Wilberforce, William 88
Williams, Betty 21
Williams, Gareth H. 68-9
Williams, Kirsty 65
Williams, Shirley 49
Wilson, Harold 13, 15, 17, 20-1, 22, 25, 28, 41, 48, 54, 83, 87, 99, 105, 135
Windsor, Roger 40
Winston Smith (*Nineteen Eighty-Four*) 4
women/women's rights 18, 48-9, 119
Women: A World Report (UN) 81
Woolwich murder (22 May 2013) 58-9, 140
Workers' Revolutionary Party (UK) 23
Working Tax Credit 50-1
World Crisis, The (Churchill) 33
Wright, Peter 23, 41

Yugoslavia 26

Zasulich, Vera 19
Z Cars 14
Zimbabwe 114, 119